CAR BUYER'S AND LEASER'S NEGOTIATING BIBLE

W. JAMES BRAGG

RANDOM HOUSE

NEW YORK

This is a completely revised and retypeset updated version of *In the Driver's Seat* by W. J. Bragg, published by Random House, Inc., in 1993.

Library of Congress Cataloging-in-Publication Data

Bragg, W. James (William James)
    Car buyer's and leaser's negotiating Bible / W. J. Bragg — 1st
ed.
      p.   cm.
    Rev. ed. of: In the driver's seat.
    Includes index.
    ISBN 0-679-76975-7 (alk. paper)
    1. Automobiles—Purchasing.   2. Automobile leasing and renting.
3. Negotiation.   I. Bragg, W. James (William James). In the
driver's seat. II. Title.
TL162.B7297   1996
629.222'029'7—dc20   95-44478
                                                      CIP

Typeset and printed in the United States of America

First Edition

9 8 7 6 5 4 3 2

New York   Toronto   London   Sydney   Auckland

DEDICATION

- To every man who's ever bought a new car or truck and wondered whether the next guy got the same vehicle for a lot less.

- To every woman who's suffered through the purchase process and wondered whether she was a victim of gender-based price discrimination.

- To every member of a minority group who's wondered whether he or she has encountered race-based price discrimination when buying a new car or truck.

- To everyone who's about to buy that first new vehicle and wonders whether he or she will end up asking the same questions.

This book is for all of you. After reading it, you'll wonder why no one ever told you this before.

Contents

Introduction   **ix**

1. **Everybody's Problem: An Uneven Playing Field**   **1**

The problem we all face in the negotiation process. The objective: to make you more knowledgeable than the salesman.

2. **The Other Problem: Price Discrimination**   **5**

The evidence that women and minorities are charged more. The most probable explanation for it. The light in the tunnel.

3. **The Big Picture**   **11**

How an overview of the current sales and inventory picture for the make and model you want can enhance your bargaining position.

4. **Attitude Adjustment**   **15**

A look at the attitudes you must adopt to shop and negotiate successfully: Psychology 101, Anatomy 101 and Reality 101.

5. **The Juggler**   **18**

The three areas where car stores make profits on the transaction. How the salesman works to prevent you from focusing on them individually.

6. **If You Haven't Got a Plan, You Haven't Got a Prayer**   **20**

The 80/20 Rule of Life. How most people buy cars. How smart shoppers avoid the sad fate of most people.

7. **Divide and Conquer**   **24**

The reason most people get too little for their trade-in. How to avoid leaving $1,000 to $2,000 on the dealer's table.

8. The Wholesale Truth, and Nothing But **27**

How to learn what your car is really worth to the dealer.
(That number is not in any book.)

9. Who Needs a Middleman? **31**

How to get top dollar by selling your used car yourself.

10. Auto Financing 101 **37**

Expanding your financing options so that you can evaluate
whether the dealer's financing is an attractive alternative.

11. The Fine Art of Shopping Without Buying **46**

How to gather the information necessary to narrow your choices
without getting stuck in a negotiating session before you're ready.

12. Saturn: A Different Kind of Deal **54**

GM's Saturn subsidiary may make a great little car. Here's why
they won't make you a great deal.

13. One-Price, "No-Dicker" Dealers: Oasis or Mirage? **59**

The emergence of dealers adopting a no-negotiation price strategy,
trying to ape Saturn's success. Why there's less in it for the buyer
than you might like. And why "no-dicker" pricing is unlikely to
become standard industry practice.

14. Learn the Cost or Pay the Price **65**

Uncovering the real dealer cost of the vehicle you want to buy,
using dealer invoice pricing, factory-to-dealer incentives, plus an
element affecting nine out of ten vehicles sold that nobody talks
about.

15. Timing Is Money **81**

The pivotal importance of timing in today's automotive market.
How to time your purchase to maximize your savings.

16. The Games Salesmen Play   88

Learning the tricks salesmen use to try to control the negotiating session and the appropriate responses to neutralize them.

17. Back-End Options: Just Say No   93

How to avoid buying things you don't need: "The Mop 'n Glow" and other marginal but expensive add-ons they'll try to sell you.

18. Are Extended Warranties Warranted?   99

How to determine whether you should buy an extended warranty contract.

19. Choosing Your Dealer Finalists   104

How to choose the dealers you'll negotiate with. Why price is no longer the only criterion.

20. Showtime!   112

How to negotiate the deal: what to do and say, and when to do and say it. Finalizing the deal without unpleasant last-minute surprises.

21. The Leasing Alternative: Breaking the Language Barrier   127

The basics of leasing demystified. Determining whether leasing makes sense for you. How to negotiate a favorable lease without letting the salesman use the "boomfog" of leasing terminology to juggle you into a high-profit deal. How to do the arithmetic to check the monthly payment figure they're trying to sell you.

22. There Must Be an Easier Way!   146

Other ways to accomplish the same objective, from doing-it-yourself by phone or fax to hiring a stand-in. Why auto brokers may not be the best answer.

23. Resisting the Final Temptation   155

The pre-ownership inspection. All the things to go over while they still own the car, before you give them the final check and sign the delivery receipt.

24. Call 1-800-288-1134 159

How to get— directly from us, quickly and easily— the specific information package you need to negotiate from a position of strength for the vehicle you want: the most recent dealer invoice pricing, details of manufacturer incentives in effect (including factory-to-dealer cash programs), and an updated overview of how the vehicle is doing in the marketplace, including a feel for actual transaction prices among knowledgeable shoppers.

25. The Executive Summary 169

A brief reminder of the major points covered in the book, with appropriate referrals to the relevant chapters.

Appendix 173

If a little knowledge is dangerous,
where are those who have so much
as to be out of danger?
—Thomas Huxley

Among new car buyers, it's those
who've read this book.

Introduction

f another book covered the subject well, we wouldn't have written this one—neither the initial edition nor this updated, expanded version. The automobile business has changed dramatically in recent years. The *Car Buyer's and Leaser's Negotiating Bible* is loaded with inside information that will empower you in today's automotive market—much of it information you won't find in any other book. And we've learned a great deal of the additional information in this edition from the actual shopping experiences of the thousands of Fighting Chance customers we've talked to. This gives us an unfair advantage over those other books—and you an unfair advantage over those car salesmen.

OUR SUBJECT IS MONEY, NOT CARS

There's an old maxim that applies here. We call it Life's 80/20 Rule. Simply stated, it says that 20 percent of the people account for 80 percent of the activity, no matter what the subject. (For example, 20 percent of moviegoers buy 80 percent of the tickets; 20 percent of readers buy 80 percent of the books.)

When the subject is the money dealers make from selling new cars, the rule says that 20 percent of the customers account for 80 percent of the profits. And when we walk into that showroom, every car salesman views every one of us as a prime candidate to join that unfortunate group. This book's reason-for-being is to keep you out of that group.

The one sure way for anyone to avoid getting taken is to become an informed and disciplined shopper, period. This book can help you become that shopper. We will *not* be steering you to any specific car or truck. *You* are the best judge of which vehicles fit your requirements. Do you like the way the vehicle looks? Is your body comfortable in that seat? Do you like the car's handling characteristics? Is it big enough for your needs? Is it too noisy, or too quiet? Some of these are very personal questions, and many are quite subjective.

And we are not experts on fuel economy, or safety, or reliability, or maintenance and repair costs, or insurance ratings. These important issues are well covered in lots of all-purpose books and magazines.

Our focus here is primarily on the elements impacting the *financial* outcome of the purchase process—elements those all-purpose books and magazines cover only superficially. Our job is to provide you with the knowledge that will give you real negotiating leverage in a transaction that traditionally has been stacked against the buyer.

We'll do that by bringing together all the relevant information, distilling and synthesizing it into one coherent presentation. We'll demystify the automotive purchase process thoroughly (in English, not AutoSpeak) and teach you how to use that information to negotiate from a position of strength, in the driver's seat.

SEVERAL SUBJECTS YOU'LL BE GLAD WE STUDIED

To illustrate, here are some important aspects of today's market reality— things you must know about to deal from strength, but areas no other book covers adequately.

1. Today the average vehicle has $500 to $1,000 or more built into its price for incentives—customer rebates, reduced-rate financing offers and secret factory-to-dealer incentives. Since you'll pay for them, you ought to be informed so that you can benefit from them.

2. Recent research shows that, compared to Caucasian males, women and minorities, who buy more than half of all new cars, face significant price discrimination in the purchase process—discrimination that may cost them over a billion dollars a year. This book presents these research results in Chapter 2 and proceeds to teach its readers how to turn the tables. (No other book we've seen even mentions this landmark study.)

3. The fortunes of auto companies and their dealers ebb and flow from month to month, impacting price flexibility for each make and model. Disappointing sales typically lead to excess inventories and a greater willingness to deal. Chapter 3 explains this in detail, and Chapter 24 provides a mechanism for you to get a current sales and inventory picture to help you identify the more vulnerable makes.

4. In this supercompetitive auto market, there's one thing no dealer wants you to know: Most dealers make several slim-profit deals every month with knowledgeable customers. In Chapters 14 and 20, you'll learn why that's true and how you can turn those reasons to your advantage. We'll even give you some overall target price guidelines for cars in different price ranges.

5. Leasing now accounts for a major percentage of passenger car purchases. Other books dismiss leasing as a bad idea unless you qualify for tax write-offs or have more money than time. *That's dated advice.* With manufacturer-subsidized offers, leasing can be a very attractive alternative for almost any creditworthy buyer. Chapter 21 is, hands down, today's bible on leasing.

6. The success of GM's Saturn division has encouraged many other dealers to adopt Saturn's one-price, "no-dicker" sales policy. But these Saturn wannabes don't have Saturn's crucial pricing umbrella working for them, and they don't offer the consumer the same pricing reassurance. Chapters 12 and 13 take you behind the curtain for a revealing look at how "no-dicker" pricing really works.

7. The Customer Satisfaction Index (CSI), a relatively new advertising staple for makes that score well in national surveys, also has implications for your shopping behavior. Manufacturers now conduct surveys to rate each of their dealers on customer satisfaction, and you should want to buy from a dealer with an above-average CSI score. Chapter 19 teaches you how to identify those dealers.

Our objective is to make this the most comprehensive, interesting and useful information package available for helping new-car and -truck shoppers save money. We won't talk down to you or tell you things you already know (such as, Dress comfortably but conservatively when visiting showrooms). We'll just explain, as simply as we can, how the process works, and how you can take advantage of it, instead of letting it take advantage of you.

COMPLETING THE LOOP: FIGHTING CHANCE®, A UNIQUE INFORMATION SERVICE

To negotiate successfully, you'll need the most current, vehicle-specific information for the cars or trucks on your short list. When you're ready, our company, Fighting Chance, offers you an easy way to get that data by calling an 800 number or writing to us, if you wish. The Fighting Chance information package contains the factory invoice pricing for the vehicle or vehicles you're shopping, a current report on manufacturers' incentive programs (including factory-to-dealer cash offers), and an updated sales and inventory picture for each make—including vehicle-specific pricing targets based on the feedback we've received on actual transaction prices from thousands of Fighting Chance customers. See Chapter 24 for ordering details.

In a time of turbulence and change, it is more true than ever that knowledge is power.
—John F. Kennedy

Everybody's Problem: An Uneven Playing Field

 uick! Can you name three things that are more fun than driving home in a brand-new car or truck? For most people, that's a tough call.

Now, can you name three things that are less fun than shopping for and negotiating the price of that new car or truck? For most people, that's even tougher.

We all suffer world-class anxiety in this process, with good reason. For years, car prices have been going up much faster than take-home pay. The average new car's actual transaction price is now over $20,000. That's more than six months' wages for a typical household, enough to make *anyone* anxious. And there's no relief in sight.

Despite evidence that "sticker shock" is hurting new car sales, you can expect the automakers to continue hiking prices. If the increases for General Motors, Ford and Chrysler averaged only a "modest" 3 percent, that would be more than $600 a year.

We can't look to the Japanese manufacturers to hold the line on prices, for two reasons. First, the political pressure to avoid escalating U.S. trade tension has forced them to shift their focus from increasing market share to increasing profits. Which means increasing prices, probably in the range of 4 to 6 percent per year. The second factor is the increased strength of the Japanese yen in relation to the U.S. dollar. In the mid-eighties, they took home over 200 yen for each dollar earned here, but a decade later the exchange rate had dropped to under 100 yen per dollar. As this international monetary relationship fluctuates, there will be periodic pressure on the Japanese to increase prices to offset the effect of a weaker dollar.

The domestic makes should see this as an opportunity to gain a pricing advantage and recapture market share from the Japanese. But Detroit's pattern has been to use the Japanese increases as an excuse to raise prices and reduce incentive offers on domestic cars.

What's the prognosis for the consumer? *The cost of the average new car will continue to increase by at least 4 to 5 percent a year.* Is it any wonder that many of us would rather visit a dentist for root canal work than visit a showroom to shop for a new car or truck?

THE REAL PROBLEM: AN UNEVEN PLAYING FIELD

The gut-level issue, of course, is that the price of that expensive machine is negotiable, and therefore different for each buyer. By contrast, the price of just about everything else we buy is firmly established, and therefore the same for each buyer. That puts the pressure on us. We've got to do something we're not used to doing: negotiate the price of the second most expensive purchase most of us will ever make. And we're operating on unfamiliar turf, in a position of weakness, because we do it only once every few years.

But those salesmen we have to negotiate with are on very familiar turf, the car store, and in a position of strength, because they do it every day. (Yes, they call the dealership "the store." There are more than 22,000 of them nationally, and the average store for a Top Six automotive brand moves 500 to 900 new cars and trucks each year. Many sell thousands!)

Those salesmen are trained to do one thing really well: maximize the car store's profit on each sale by separating us from as much money as possible. Their job is to determine how much is "as much as possible" for each prospect and, if the number is high enough, to close the sale at that price before the prospect gets away.

We make that job easier than it should be by giving them lots of important information they can use. We tell them exactly which car we want, and how much we can pay per month, and which vehicle we're trading in. In return, they give us no information we can use, such as how much that car really cost them, how low they'll really go to sell it, and what our trade-in is really worth. As a result, a playing field that was uneven from the start tips even further toward them. And when the transaction is over, most of us don't know whether we got a good deal or got taken.

EVERYONE DESERVES A FIGHTING CHANCE

As a *Motor Trend* writer said in an annual auto review issue, "Negotiating with terrorists is easier than bargaining with car dealers." That's why we wrote this book. We wanted to give the average new-vehicle shopper a fighting chance by making the playing field a little more level.

Our goal is to make the purchase process less painful and costly for you. To do that, we must change something important in that process. Since we can't change those salesmen and what they do, we've got to help change you and what you do.

THE OBJECTIVE: TO MAKE YOU MORE KNOWLEDGEABLE THAN THE CAR SALESMAN

That's not Mission Impossible. The average car salesman isn't that knowledgeable. He's trained to qualify, control and close most of the people who walk in, prospects who just don't know much. But he's not well prepared to control and close people with solid knowledge of his business, a well-planned, disciplined approach and insights that even he may not understand. Those shoppers can have real negotiating leverage.

(Incidentally, when we say salesmen, assume we mean both sexes. There are successful auto saleswomen, but the male stereotype is still the dominant factor. Also, when we say cars, assume we're referring to both cars and trucks.)

How can we make you more knowledgeable than the car salesman? By giving you the attitude, facts, up-to-date insights and advice you need to negotiate from a position of greater strength.

We can't guarantee, of course, that you'll save hundreds or thousands more with this information than without it. That's up to you and what you do with it. The supply and demand conditions in your market for the vehicles you're interested in will also influence the outcome.

But remember, knowledge is power. The main advantage the salesman has over most buyers is that he thinks he's got all the knowledge. If you absorb the information we give you, you'll know more than most car salesmen. If you act on this information, you'll go into the process with real confidence in your ability to negotiate effectively. And if you believe you can, you will.

NO PAIN, NO GAIN

Most people work harder planning a $2,000 vacation than planning the purchase of the $20,000 car they'll be vacationing in for years. Why? For two reasons: (1) Planning a vacation is more fun; and (2) they know how to plan a vacation, but they don't know how to shop for a car. If smart shopping were easy, everyone would do it.

The facts say everyone doesn't. Incredible as it seems, in a national survey conducted by the Dohring Company of Glendale, California, *one out of seven prospective new-car buyers was not aware that new-vehicle prices were negotiable!* And we'd bet that most of the other six frequently pay more than they realize, simply because they aren't focused on all the ways a car store can make money on a deal. (More on this in Chapter 5.)

Smart shopping requires homework. Studying this book and acting on it intelligently will require more of your time than simply going out and buying a car next Saturday. The trade-off is between time and money, perhaps as much as several thousand dollars.

We'll assume that you wouldn't have bought this book if you weren't willing to trade time for money. Let's get on with your education.

Everything is funny as long as it is happening to someone else.

—Will Rogers

The Other Problem: Price Discrimination

Our civil rights laws focus on the areas of employment, education, housing and public accommodations. When it comes to the prices we pay for the things we buy, there's a comfortable assumption that good old American competition at the retail level tends to eliminate price discrimination.

Try telling that to women, who know they pay more for shoes than men do for theirs, even when the materials and workmanship are the same. Or to inner-city residents, who know that stores in their neighborhoods often charge higher prices for lower-quality goods than similar stores elsewhere.

Women and minorities will not be surprised to learn that they also face significant price discrimination in the automotive marketplace. *We believe a conservative estimate of the cost of this discrimination is over a billion dollars a year, compared to the prices paid for the same vehicles by white males.*

WOMEN MAKE THE WHEELS GO ROUND

The female working population has grown dramatically over the last few decades, sparking a revolution in auto design and marketing strategies. With three out of four women between twenty and fifty-four years old in the labor force, women have become a key target for automakers.

Manufacturers now spend as much money researching women's automotive needs as men's, with good reason. Women purchase half of the new passenger cars sold and more than one third of the light trucks, including some very profitable segments (such as minivans like the Dodge Caravan and sport-utility vehicles like the Jeep Grand Cherokee).

Many vehicles are designed to appeal primarily to women. Female designers play important roles at automobile companies. They frequently supervise new-vehicle design teams, especially for sporty coupes—a market segment aimed directly at women which includes the Honda Prelude, Mitsubishi Eclipse, Toyota Celica, Acura Integra and the convertible Volkswagen Cabriolet.

The auto manufacturers have changed their ways to satisfy the needs of this powerful new economic force; they treat women differently from men. As a result, both win. Women get the products they want, and manufacturers sell more new cars and trucks.

The automakers' franchised *dealers,* however, are another story. Most women have always suspected that new-car salesmen treat them differently than men and that, as a result, they end up paying a different price from men—a higher price. That's why many of them drag along their husbands, boyfriends or fathers when they shop.

Many members of minority groups have suspected they face similar price discrimination.

Now there's irrefutable evidence that substantiates these suspicions.

THE SEARCH FOR THE SMOKING GUN

Ian Ayres, a professor at Stanford Law School and a research fellow of the American Bar Foundation, was interested in testing the ability of competitive market forces to eliminate gender- and race-based price discrimination in markets not covered by civil rights laws. Since a new-car purchase represents a large investment for most consumers, he saw the retail automobile market as "particularly ripe for scrutiny."

Between the summers of 1988 and 1990, when he was an associate professor at the Northwestern University School of Law, he conducted research to examine whether women and minorities were at a disadvantage in the process of negotiating the price of a new car.

He trained several college-educated testers of different genders and races to negotiate in the same way for specific models. They conducted 180 independent negotiations at 90 dealerships in the Chicago area, bargaining to each dealer's "final cash offer." To eliminate other financial considerations, no trade-in vehicles were involved.

THE FACTS OF PRICE DISCRIMINATION

The smoking gun wasn't hard to find. The results were published as the *Harvard Law Review*'s lead article in February 1991. They demonstrated that retail car dealerships systematically offered substantially better prices on identical cars to white men than they did to white women and African-Americans.

Specifically, final offers to white women contained about 40 percent more dealer profit than final offers to white men. Offers to African-American men contained more than twice the profit, and African-American women had to pay more than three times the markup of white male testers.

The tendency to charge African-Americans higher prices was echoed in this comment one dealer made to Professor Ayres: "My cousin owns a dealership in a black neighborhood. He doesn't sell nearly as many [cars], but he hits an awful lot of home runs. You know, sometimes it seems like the people that can least afford it have to pay the most."

The study also revealed that testers were systematically steered to salespeople of their own race and gender, who then gave them *worse* deals than others received from salespeople of a different race and gender. (Consumers tend to feel more comfortable with someone of their own race and gender; salespeople take advantage of that implied trust and sell them higher-profit deals.)

The major conclusions of this initial study were confirmed by a subsequent larger-scale test involving four hundred additional negotiations in the Chicago area.

Years have passed since this research was completed, and you might wonder whether the result would be different if the study were conducted today. Based on our personal contacts with thousands of new car shoppers each year, there is no evidence of significant changes. It would be easier to U-turn a supertanker in the Panama Canal than to change the way car salesmen operate.

GENDER DISCRIMINATION GETS A THEME SONG

On the assumption that our female readers have a sense of humor about this, we'd like to share the lyrics to a little song parody we've written. It's sung to the tune of that old standard, "I Found a Million-Dollar Baby at the Five-and-Ten Cent Store." We call it "I Made a Bundle on the Lady When I Put Her in a New Car." Imagine all those chauvinist car salesmen at their annual convention, hoisting their glasses to toast their male prowess and singing these lyrics:

> She was my lucky April shopper,
> It was my chance to be a star.
> I made a bundle on the lady
> When I put her in a new car.

> She thought she'd be here half an hour,
> We kept her here for three or four.
> We made a bundle on that lady
> With the deal she got at our store!

> She wanted basic transportation
> But much to her surprise,
> She drove home in a sports car
> With payments twice the size!

> So if you're looking for a bargain
> Our showroom isn't very far.
> I'll make a bundle on you, baby,
> When I put you in a new car!

THE IMPLICIT ASSUMPTIONS BEHIND THE FACTS

Professor Ayres hypothesizes an explanation for this price discrimination. While there's no way to prove it, we think he's right on the money. Here's the essence of his reasoning:

- The dealer's objective is to maximize profits on each sale. (That's the American way, right?)

- The natural outcome of the bargaining process is that identical vehicles are sold to different buyers at different prices. Dealers make little or no profit on some sales, but a great deal of profit on others.

- The less the competition with other dealers for a given sale, the more profit the dealer is likely to make on the transaction.

- If a dealership can infer that some prospects are less likely to shop at other dealerships—because they aren't well informed about the dynamics of the retail automotive marketplace, or because they can't spend the time required, or because they simply hate the entire bargaining process and just want to get it behind them—that dealership is more likely to view these prospects as potential patsies for high-margin transactions. And that dealership is more likely to conclude that it can safely charge these prospects higher prices.

- Like it or not, our society is still rife with stereotypes about women and minority groups that provide at least a subconscious rationale for salespeople to view them as more likely candidates for high-margin, slam-dunk, sucker deals. Here are the most obvious:

> *Women and minorities have less time to shop around for competitive bids.* Compared to white men, they are less likely to be able to take time off from work to shop without losing wages. And women are more likely to have family responsibilities that further restrict their shopping time.

> *Women and minorities are less sophisticated about the auto shopping process.* They are less likely to seek out information about the realities of the retail market and to understand that the sticker price is negotiable. They will be more passive in the sales situation, less likely to negotiate aggressively. That will make it easier for the salesperson to control the outcome.

> *Women, in general, are more averse to the entire bargaining process.* Haggling over the price of a new vehicle is a competitive ordeal. Some men relish the battle; for them it's one of the last macho things they can do without a gun. Most women simply hate it. They'll pay a higher cost just to get it behind them.

THE LIGHT IN THE TUNNEL

Women and minority readers shouldn't be discouraged by these revelations. The purpose of this exercise is to get into the opponent's brain, to understand what's in there. The good news is, that's just about all that's in there.

And is the salesman going to be surprised when he meets you! Because you're going to shake his faith in those implicit assumptions, confusing him and neutralizing his offense. He'll try all his tricks, but you'll be that knowledgeable, disciplined shopper we promised you'd become, and they won't work.

The road from here to there begins on the next page. It's straight and clearly marked.

An IBM sales representative in Milwaukee contracted with a dealer to buy a new Dodge Viper, Chrysler's limited-production sports car, for $2,500 over the suggested retail price. When the vehicle arrived, the dealer sued the customer to get out of the contract. According to The Wall Street Journal, *he thought he could sell it for as much as $20,000 over the sticker price! On learning of this embarrassing incident, Chrysler's executive vice president for sales and marketing lamented, "We have to change the entire culture of our franchise."*

The

Big

Picture

Any deal you make will be influenced by two things that have nothing to do with you: the overall state of the automobile market, and the specific supply and demand conditions for the vehicle you want.

Since the auto sales climate is one of the most overreported subjects in journalism, getting up to speed starts with simply keeping your eyes and ears open. As you think about new cars or trucks, pay attention to those monthly sales reports on the TV news, in your local paper, or in national media like *The Wall Street Journal* or *USA Today.* They'll give you a general feel for how eager dealers are to sell new vehicles.

What you really want to know, however, is how eager some specific manufacturers and dealers might be to sell the vehicles you're interested in buying.

THEIR WEAKNESS IS YOUR OPPORTUNITY

The retail automobile business is driven by momentum, both in the overall market and the fortunes of each specific make. Over a period of years the market runs in cycles, from hot to lukewarm to cold and back again. Within each cycle, there are winners and losers among both manufacturers and specific models. Some automakers watch their sales and market shares wither, while others develop the tough competitor's ability to weather any storm.

The smart shopper understands that these differences create buying opportunities, and that you should be able to negotiate a better deal with those who are most eager to sell.

LEARN HOW THEY'RE DOING

There is real power in knowing how the makes and models you are interested in are doing in the marketplace. Is their sales performance better or worse than their key competitors' and the total market? Are their inventory levels relatively higher? As a general rule, dealers selling makes that are doing less well, with higher inventories, will be more willing to deal aggressively on price than those selling makes with relatively better sales and lower inventories. Automakers with poor sales are also more likely to offer customer and/or dealer incentives.

For perspective, industrywide inventory levels tend to fluctuate throughout the year in a range from roughly a 55-day supply to about a 75-day supply. For most manufacturers a two-month supply is an ideal target, providing the vast majority of buyers with sufficient color and equipment choices. Inventories higher than that usually increase costs much more than they do sales. Whenever they approach the three-month level, you can bet that the costs of financing that supply are hurting both the manufacturers and their dealers. Those makes should be more vulnerable to smart, informed shoppers.

Here's a comparison of two vehicles to illustrate the point:

- One car's sales are running 38 percent below previous annual levels. The average dealer is selling just one each month. And on the first of the month, there was a whopping 120-day supply in inventory.

• A directly competitive car of another make has sales 5 percent ahead of last year's level. The average dealer sells 15 each month. And there was a 42-day supply in inventory on the first of the month.

Given the relative sales and inventory positions of these two vehicles, which dealers are likely to be more flexible on price? The ones selling the first car, naturally.

Where can you find the information you need to understand the current status of the makes and models you are considering? Visit a large public library and ask to see the most recent issues of *Automotive News,* the industry's weekly newspaper. Many big libraries subscribe to this publication, which prints the most recent sales and inventory data in successive issues each month, by make and model.

It's also helpful to know the number of franchised dealers for each make, shown in the table below. This enables you to analyze sales figures to determine how many of each model the average dealer sells each month. That

Make	No. of Dealers*	Make	No. of Dealers*
Acura	285	Land Rover	90
Audi	280	Lexus	170
BMW	350	Lincoln	1,625
Buick	2,855	Mazda	905
Cadillac	1,580	Mercedes-Benz	360
Chevrolet	4,440	Mercury	2,640
Chrysler	2,940	Mitsubishi	510
Dodge	2,900	Nissan	1,245
Eagle	2,170	Oldsmobile	2,990
Ford	4,255	Plymouth	2,930
Geo	4,040	Pontiac	2,885
GMC	2,455	Porsche	205
Honda	995	Saab	280
Hyundai	490	Saturn	350
Infiniti	155	Subaru	675
Isuzu	585	Suzuki	320
Jaguar	125	Toyota	1,365
Jeep	2,170	Volkswagen	625
		Volvo	380

*These numbers tend to remain relatively constant. In bad times, some dealers go out of business; in good times, manufacturers add a few franchises.

knowledge will often strengthen your confidence by confirming that it's a lot easier for you to find someone who wants to sell one than for them to find someone who wants to buy one.

When you're ready for serious negotiating, you should know that there is an easier way to get the current sales and inventory picture for the makes and models you are considering, along with the data on the current dealer invoice price of the vehicle or vehicles, and an up-to-date listing of manufacturers' incentives for both the customer and the dealer. See Chapter 24 for details.

Necessity never made a good bargain.

—Benjamin Franklin

Attitude

Adjustment

Here are three basic principles of automotive negotiating that you must burn into your brain. Think of them as three legs of the stool that will transform you attitudinally from a potential pushover into a tower of strength.

PSYCHOLOGY 101

This is a serious competition. It may seem relatively civilized, but it's definitely you against them.

One of the primary rules of this competition: Don't give your opponent a psychological advantage. That's exactly what you'll do as soon as you show him that you're emotionally attached to any specific vehicle. As soon as he knows that, he's dealing from a position of greater strength. And you'll end up paying more for the car simply because he knows you have to have it.

Car salesmen are trained to make the purchase process as emotional as possible. Decades of experience have confirmed that they get more money from emotional people than from cool, rational shoppers.

How do you avoid this trap? *By projecting total emotional detachment.*

In the showroom, on the lot and during the test drive your behavior should say, A car is a car, something that gets me from Point A to Point B. Lots of cars will do that, including many that this store doesn't even sell. I'm going to check them all out and buy the best deal.

(Ask your friends who shop for antiques about the "Don't-let-'em-know-what-you-really-want-as-soon-as-you-walk-in" rule. They'll tell you it also works well at estate sales, swap meets and garage sales.)

That doesn't mean you can't fall in love. Just don't let the salesman know until you've completed the transaction. At your price, not his.

> HEAVY BREATHING SHOULD BE RESERVED FOR MORE APPROPRIATE OCCASIONS. IN CAR STORES IT LEADS ONLY TO HEAVY PAYMENTS.

ANATOMY 101

Look down at the floor right now. That's where you'll find the most powerful negotiating tools you'll ever own: your feet.

The only thing a car salesman dreads more than selling you a car too cheaply is watching you walk out of his store, into the arms of another salesman at another store. He's got bags of tricks to keep you there for hours. (Dealers sometimes *require* that their salesmen *not let you leave* without seeing a sales manager!)

If you think you're being pressured, or he's not listening to you and moving in the direction you want, tell him politely that he's wasting your time . . . and leave. (A funny thing happens if you walk; it actually *improves* your leverage when you return later, because he'll know you're someone who'll walk again if things aren't going your way.)

> ONE REASON GOD GAVE YOU FEET WAS TO WALK AWAY FROM CAR SALESMEN.

REALITY 101

Pick up any buyer's guide to this year's models, and you will find a mind-boggling offering of new cars and trucks. There are many more choices than any civilized society needs to get around town. That's because the people who run car companies are terminal optimists who believe that if they build them we will buy them—all of them. They eventually learn, painfully, that building them is easy, but selling them is hard. Then they are fired and replaced by a new crop of terminal optimists.

Reality is that there will be more car production capacity than car buying capacity for as long as anyone can see into the future. We'd have to take the minimum driving age down to three years old for all the manufacturers to realize the sales projections they made when they built their production facilities.

Reality is that it will always be much easier for you to find someone who wants to sell a new car than for a car salesman to find someone who wants to buy one.

Trust this reality.

> REALITY IS THAT YOU CAN WALK AWAY FROM ANY DEAL, OR ANY CAR, AND BE ABSOLUTELY CERTAIN THERE IS ONE JUST LIKE IT, AND PROBABLY BETTER, AROUND THE CORNER.

The time is long overdue for this industry—the largest and most important industry in the world—to erase the popular idea that its No. 1 priority is to pull the wool over everyone's eyes.

—From an editorial by the publisher of *Automotive News*

The

Juggler

When you're buying a new car, the salesman has three balls in the air, three important areas of opportunity to make money on the transaction.

• First, he can make money on the front end, on the difference between your purchase price and the dealer's cost on that new vehicle.

• Second, he can make money on the back end, selling you things like financing (with related life and disability insurance), extended warranty coverage, and dealer add-on options like rustproofing and fabric protection.

• Third, if the deal includes your trade-in vehicle, he can make money on the difference between what the car store really pays for your car and what they get for it, either by retailing it through their own used-car department or by wholesaling it to a used-car dealer.

(If it surprises you to learn that there's more profit potential in the second and third areas than in the first, you are in the group that needs this book the most.)

Think of the salesman as a juggler, trained to keep all these balls moving so fast that you can't tell which is which.

He wants to make a good profit on all three if he can. But the total gross is what counts, and there isn't a dealer alive who wouldn't give up profit on one of these balls to swing a deal if he knew he could make a killing on the other two.

The world is full of naive-but-happy car buyers who think they got a great deal because they bought "below dealer invoice." Or because they got a "fabulous trade-in allowance." Or a "big discount" on an extended warranty policy.

They watched only the ball that they were interested in. But the salesman watched them all.

We'll cover how to watch . . . and even control . . . what happens with each of these balls. But first you need an overall shopping plan.

YES, VIRGINIA, THERE IS A BETTER WAY

Smart buyers don't rely on car salesmen for any important information. They don't give them any, either. Smart buyers have a shopping plan that reverses the sequence that most people follow:

• They start by focusing on the car they've got. They know they're either going to sell it themselves or trade it in, and that the proceeds will represent an important part of the new car's down payment. So they begin by finding out how much their vehicle is really worth in their market today, both at retail and at wholesale.

• Then they decide whether they'll sell it themselves at retail or trade it in at wholesale. (They know the difference will affect the money available for their down payment.)

• Then they turn to the essential financial questions. They decide on the monthly payment they can handle comfortably, including auto insurance, which costs a lot more for new cars than for old ones. They also determine the down payment they can afford. They know that bigger is better, so they find some loose cash to add to what they'll get for their current car.

• They take all this information and shop for money before they shop seriously for a car or truck. This gives them a good fix on the maximum amount they can pay for a new vehicle, including all the miscellaneous sales taxes and license fees that many salesmen don't mention until you're committed to a price for the car. It also provides a basis for measuring the attractiveness of the financing offered by the dealer or manufacturer.

• They study the advantages and disadvantages of leasing versus buying and decide whether they are candidates to lease. If they are, they do additional homework to understand the key elements of leasing, including exactly how to do the arithmetic to determine the monthly payment.

• Concurrently, they're reading articles on the vehicles they're interested in for information to help narrow their choices, and they're visiting car stores to obtain brochures and take test drives. But they make it clear from the start that they are not going to buy on those visits, and they avoid getting into any salesman's "closing room" because they know they're not ready.

• They decide on at least two or three finalists, including the trim levels and optional equipment they'd like on each. They pick their first-choice vehicle and at least one attractive fallback alternative, based on both emotional appeal and rational analysis.

• Next, they gather all the information they can about what those vehicles actually cost the dealer, including the impact of any current factory-to-dealer incentives, as a basis from which to negotiate a purchase price confidently and aggressively. They also bone up on any direct consumer incentives being offered by the manufacturers.

• They do a little additional homework to determine which dealer finalists they want to approach in the negotiation stage. They recognize that some car stores can be much better places to buy than others, for reasons that have little to do with price.

• With solid knowledge of the real wholesale and retail values of their current cars, the best financing they can arrange independently and the actual dealer costs of the vehicles they want most, they plan the best way to approach several car stores with an aggressive offer.

• They understand the potential value of proper timing, especially in relation to incentive programs, and they plan their approach accordingly.

• They review the basic tricks salesmen are likely to use to boost their store's profits, including all the high-cost/low-value add-on options they'll try to sell, and they are ready to handle them.

• Then, and only then, are they ready to present themselves to car salesmen as serious prospects.

• Finally, they go into the negotiating process determined to let the guys at the car store do the stewing. They know that those guys need us more than we need them.

For typical buyers, the serious shopping phase takes an average of about five weeks, from the time they start visiting car stores for test drives until the day they drive a new car home.

Following the smart buyers' lead, let's focus now on the car you drive today. We'll start with an illustration of what can happen when you don't keep a close eye on that ball.

7

Training is everything. The peach was once a bitter almond; cauliflower is nothing but cabbage with a college education.

—Mark Twain

Divide

and

Conquer

R ead the next paragraph twice.

Even if you're the world's worst price negotiator, the car store probably will make more profit selling your clean, well-maintained trade-in to someone else than it will make selling a new car or truck to you. *And that profit will come directly out of your pocket.*

It's a fact. Today the average dealer makes more profit selling used than new cars for two reasons: simple economics and simple new-car buyers.

THE SIMPLE ECONOMICS

New-car pricing is supercompetitive because every dealer has essentially the same merchandise to sell at the same price. A new Chevy Cavalier is the same car, with the same sticker price, at every Chevy store in town. In addition, new cars carry more overhead, from fancy showrooms to higher inventory financing costs. That makes it even more difficult to sell them for big profits.

By contrast, all used cars are different from one another, even when they're the same year, make and model. With no standardized sticker prices or dealer invoice costs and no easy way to measure their condition, especially that of the important parts under the hood, it's more difficult for consumers to evaluate their true worth. That makes it relatively easy for car stores to sell every one of them at a profit.

THE SIMPLE NEW-CAR BUYER

The key to a dealer's used-car profit is the new-car buyer. Two out of three deals include a trade-in. And most people literally give away their trade-in, without understanding what they really get for it.

That's because they don't watch all the balls. Instead, they let the salesman confuse the issue by juggling the new-car sell price and the old-car buy price in a single package deal.

They may think they're getting a great deal because the trade-in allowance is $1,000 over wholesale Kelley Blue Book or some other impressive-sounding measurement. They don't realize that the juggler's deal combines that apparently attractive trade-in allowance with a much higher new-car price than they could have negotiated without a trade-in. He's simply taking money out of one of their pockets and putting it in the other. By the time they agree to the package, it's all mumbo jumbo to them, but at least part of it sounds terrific.

The car store then turns their trade-in into a nice little money machine:

• If it's in relatively good shape and they need it in their used-car inventory, they'll spend a couple of hundred dollars making it look great and retail it themselves for a profit of $1,000 to $1,500 or more. (Two of every three vehicles taken in trade are retailed by the dealership; the average new-car dealer retails over thirty used cars every month.)

• If it's in relatively poor shape, or if they don't need it, they'll take a quick $300 to $700 profit by wholesaling it the next day to a used-car dealer. (Each year, new-car dealerships wholesale over 5 million used cars to other used car dealers.)

Either way they'll probably make more money on that trade-in than on the new car they sold.

The bottom line is that customers with desirable used cars who buy this kind of trade-in allowance deal typically leave between $1,000 and $2,000 on the table.

If your car is an ugly hulk that barely wheezes onto the dealer's lot, you won't lose much by letting him take it off your hands. But if you have a clean, one-owner, average-miles-for-age vehicle that's mechanically sound, there are two ways to keep most of that money in your pocket:

- The best way is to *sell it yourself* at retail, as illustrated in Chapter 9.

- The second best way is to sell it to a dealer, but for its *true wholesale value,* as covered in the next chapter.

First, however, you must master the next rule. *It's the single most important factor to remember if you're going to succeed in this competition.*

DIVIDE AND CONQUER, COMBINE AND BE CONQUERED

The customers described here left a lot of money on the table because they let the salesman combine two elements that should never be combined: the selling price for the new vehicle and the buying price for their used vehicle. When they let him do that, they lost the ability to watch all the balls. As a result, they paid more for the new car than a smart buyer would have and received less for the old car than a smart seller would have. And they never knew either what they paid for one or what they got paid for the other.

Write this a hundred times on the blackboard of your mind:

- **BUYING A NEW CAR IS ONE DEAL.**
- **SELLING AN OLD CAR IS ANOTHER.**
- **KEEP THEM SEPARATE AND YOU'LL WIN.**
- **COMBINE THEM AND YOU'LL LOSE.**

Now let's develop the knowledge you need to keep them separate and thereby keep control of the negotiation.

It's powerful pantomime.

The skilled salesman doesn't say a word as he checks out your trade-in. His hands do the talking, lingering over every little scratch or blemish—silently, but effectively reducing the vehicle's value . . . in your mind.

Don't attend his performance. Give him the keys and wait for his return. You'll have a punch line of your own: You know what it's worth.

The
Wholesale
Truth, and
Nothing But

The only right price for your trade-in is its actual wholesale value. Unless you know that number and make the salesman aware that you do, you will get less than true wholesale, and the car store will make an extra profit selling your old car. (You will never get more than true wholesale. If they offer more, the difference is coming from your wallet, not theirs, in the form of a higher price on the new car.)

Knowing your car's true wholesale value will also help you decide whether to trade it in or sell it yourself. You'll compare that value to the retail price you can expect to get from an individual, a subject covered in the next chapter. The difference will surprise you. If you decide to trade it despite this difference, at least you'll be doing it with your eyes open.

THE TRUTH ABOUT THOSE LITTLE BOOKS

How do you discover your car's true wholesale value? Not by looking in any book—blue, black or red—because those books don't reflect the current wholesale climate for your car in your market.

Remember, every used car is different, and local conditions always affect values. Yet one of those big-name little books actually admitted to us that the numbers are exactly the same in every regional edition it publishes! (Their numbers come primarily from auto auctions. Have you or your friends ever bought or sold a car at an auto auction?)

Those books will tell you whether your car is in the $10,000 or the $15,000 ball park, but they won't tell you reliably whether it's worth $9,700 or $11,200. And numbers for the same car can differ widely from book to book. (Be aware that many salesmen will pull out a lower-priced book when they're buying a used car and a higher-priced book when they're selling it.)

There's an old saying: Nobody has a decision to make until somebody makes them an offer. Well, those little used-car pricing books don't contain any offers, and you shouldn't use them to make any decisions. To get a number you can rely on, you need some real offers.

PLAYING THE GAME

You'll get those offers by playing a little game some afternoon, shopping your used car at some of the very stores near home or work where you'll eventually be negotiating for your new car. (We're assuming that you've got a vehicle that someone might find attractive, not a heap ready for the wrecking yard.)

First, make sure your vehicle is clean and mechanically sound. Then drive it to Automobile Row. Go to dealers selling the new vehicles you're interested in, but pull into their used-car departments and ask for the person who buys used cars. Get his name and write it down.

As he approaches, remind yourself that the dealership makes more money selling used cars than new cars, and that a continuous supply of salable used cars is essential for the health of the business. Whether new-vehicle sales are up or down, franchised dealers regularly sell more used than new cars.

When consumer confidence is high and new-car sales are healthy, folks who buy used cars are likely to be trading up. When consumer confidence is depressed and new-vehicle sales are down, more people opt for used cars, but there are fewer trade-ins of the attractive one-owner cars they'd like to buy.

That means every used-car manager will always need good used cars, and it should be a seller's market for a nice, clean trade-in. If you've got one, he is very interested in buying it, no matter what he might say at first.

HERE'S THE SCRIPT

Tell him that you're planning to sell your car, you don't want the hassle of selling it yourself, you're visiting a few used-car dealers, and you'd like to know what he'd pay for it. (If he asks why you're not trading it for another, say you're buying your sister's year-old Chevy.)

He'll take the car, check it out and come back with a figure. Whatever number he gives, you should say nicely, "That sounds low to me. I got the impression from a couple of other dealers that it was worth more than that to a good used-car operation." *Then bite your tongue and wait for him to say something.*

If he says that's his final offer, you've learned what you came in for. Thank him for his time and drive to another store.

With most used-car managers, however, the first offer is typically a low-ball opener to see how easy and uninformed you are. He might increase his initial offer right away. More likely he'll ask what the other guys offered, or what you want for it.

FOLLOW THE BOUNCING BALL . . .

Remember that your objective is to find out how much higher he might go, so that you can put a realistic wholesale value on your car. Your answer to his question will depend on the "value ball park" your car is in. Here are some rough guidelines for answers that will help you get to a realistic number:

• If his offer was under $3,000 but not wildly out of line as an opener for your car, tell him that based on what you've heard elsewhere you believe the car is worth *at least $500 more.*

• If his offer was between $3,000 and $5,000, tell him that based on other dealers' comments, you believe the car is worth *at least $750 more.*

- If his offer was between $5,000 and $7,000, tell him that based on what you've heard elsewhere, you believe the car is worth *at least $1,000 more.*

You get the idea. If your car's "value ball park" is higher than these examples, raise your response accordingly.

Most important, after you respond with a "bump," bite your tongue again! Don't say another word until he says something in return.

If he says your figure is way out of line, ask him if that means his first offer was his best offer. If he says your number is high, ask him how high he thinks it is.

Chances are, he'll counter with a better number than his opener. At this point, tell him (if it's true) that you're the only owner, you've got all the maintenance records, you just had the scheduled service done last month and all it needed was new brake pads. He's not going to have to invest big bucks in fixing anything.

Then pick a number halfway between your last figure and his, tell him you think it should be worth that much to him, *and bite your tongue again.*

At this point he might say it's not worth that much, that his last offer was his best one. Or he might agree with your new number and ask if you'd sell it to him for that price.

Your answer to either response should be, "I'll certainly consider it seriously. But first I'm going to make a few more stops. How long will your offer be good?" Make a quick note of the answer, tell him you'll get back to him in the next few days, thank him for his time and head for your next stop.

However the discussion ends, you've learned your car's true wholesale value to that used-car operation. Remember, however, that one used-car department might be fully stocked and not want your car unless they can "steal" it from you at a lowball price and wholesale it to a used-car dealer for a quick, easy profit.

To get a reliable estimate, you must repeat the same drill at a couple of other new-car dealerships (including at least one selling the make of your used car, where it would be a natural addition to their inventory) and at a couple of big used-car-only dealers. Be sure to ask each of them how long their offer will be good.

You'll spend half a day doing this, but it'll pay off—especially a week later, when a salesman gives you a lowball trade-in offer for your car and you tell him that Joe Smith, *his used-car manager,* told you last week that he'd pay $1,000 more! And that's the wholesale truth.

Private individuals represent the majority of the used-car market. They've sold over $57 billion in used cars annually without taking trades, providing warranties or service.

Right or wrong, buyers will pay more for a privately owned car. Why? Trust.

—President of a consignment consulting firm that applies the real estate sales concept to the used-car market (quoted in *Automotive News*)

Who Needs a Middleman?

The best way to avoid getting used by a new-car dealer is to avoid trading in a good used car. Instead, sell it yourself to an individual. It's more work, but it pays awfully well. The difference between wholesaling it to a car store and retailing it yourself can be $1,000 to $2,000 or more for a mid-priced car in good shape. (Generally, the better the condition, the bigger the spread between wholesale and retail.)

Why give that much money to a middleman, when there's bona fide demand for what you've got to sell?

Lots of people would rather buy a clean, well-maintained, one-owner car from an individual than take a chance on something from a used-car dealer. (In fact, 54 percent of used-car sales are between private parties.) These folks think they'll get a better car for less money. Also, they typically can get the historical maintenance records from the owner, and knowing how it's been treated gives them more confidence in its worth.

This preference may be strongest among *nonsmokers,* who now number seven out of ten U.S. adults. Many of them will even pay a premium for a nicotine-free vehicle!

To get a feel for retail prices of cars like yours, it's okay to start by calling your bank or credit union to ask what the used-car book says. *But remember, that book wasn't written about your car in your market this month.* You need to do more homework.

☎ REACHING OUT:
LEARNING BY TALKING, NOT WALKING

Fortunately, you can do this homework on the phone. Check the ads in your weekend paper and in those used-car classifieds that seem to be everywhere. Call a few private sellers and ask about their cars—asking price, mileage, condition, equipment, type of driving done, and whether: (a) they're the original owner, (b) they've got the service records, (c) they've permitted smoking, and (d) the car has ever been in an accident. (Tell them you'd plan to have it checked by a mechanic who can tell.)

If it's a mid-priced car they're asking $6,000 or more for, find out how low they might really go by picking a number that's between $1,500 and $2,000 less and asking if they'd consider selling it for that price. If they refuse, bump the number in increments, starting with a couple of $500 bumps, followed by one or two $250 bumps until you find a price they'd consider. Thank them and say you'll think about it.

Then mentally compare your car with theirs to see if you think yours is worth more or less. If the cars are roughly comparable except that they're smokers and you're not, yours should be worth at least $300 more to a nonsmoking buyer, no matter what year or model.

Next, call a few new-car stores that sell your make and ask for their used-car department. Tell them that you're looking for a good, clean used car that's the year, make and model of the car you own.

• If they have one, ask about the mileage, how it's equipped, the asking price and (lastly) the color. If it's blue, tell them you want red or white and thank them. Don't give them your phone number.

- If they don't have one, tell them that you'd prefer to buy from a reputable dealer than from an unknown private party, and ask what would be a fair price. When they quote a price and say they'll find one, say you'll think about it, but you want to talk to a few more dealers. Thank them, but don't give them your phone number.

This exercise will give you a good idea of what your car is worth at retail, compared to other cars of the same year, make and model.

Based on this telephone research among private parties and used-car departments, you should be able to pick your expected price, the price you actually think you can get. Figure that this number is somewhere in the range between "realistic" dealer selling prices (probably 10 to 15 percent below their asking prices) and the prices those private parties would "consider." Then choose a *slightly higher* number for your asking price, keeping it below the used-car department's asking price.

Next, have your car detailed to make it look beautiful inside and out, have the oil changed and all the other fluids brought to the right levels, and fix any obvious engine, brake or wheel alignment problems that might shake a prospect's confidence during a test drive and kill a sale. Also make sure the radio, air conditioner, heater, defroster, lights, wipers and turn signals work.

NOW YOU'RE THE CAR SALESMAN

Now you're ready to call your newspaper and those used-car classifieds to place a weekend ad that describes the good things about your car. The hot buttons (if they're true) are one nonsmoking owner, low mileage, very clean and complete service record. The service record can be particularly reassuring to many potential buyers, since many used-car swindlers buy high-mileage cars at auctions, roll back the odometers illegally and then pose as private parties selling "pampered, one-owner cars."

Don't put a price in the ad. Just say, "MUST SELL," and add the hot buttons just listed, your phone number, and the best weekday and weekend hours to call.

When they call and ask, give them that slightly higher asking price you picked, but make it clear that you've got some flexibility. If they ask for your rock-bottom number, tell them that you haven't established one. Say that some other people are interested in the car, that it's a one-owner car that's been reliable for you, that you're sure somebody is going to like it a lot, and that you're confident you'll be able to work out an agreeable price with that person. Then ask if they'd like directions to your place and about what time you should expect them.

If they like the car when they see it but make an offer that's well below your asking price, assume that's not their final offer. Counteroffer somewhere in between, but still above the price your research said you can expect to get.

To create a greater sense of urgency and value, try the old car salesman's trick: Say you've been offered $450 more by someone who's coming back in the morning. If they really want the car, chances are good they'll raise their offer when they hear that, and your excuse for taking it will be a bird in the hand.

If they like the car but instead of making an offer they ask what your rock-bottom number is, tell them you really don't want to sell the car for much less than your asking price, that you've done a lot of comparison shopping and know that's a fair price for a clean, one-owner vehicle like yours. Then counter by shaving a couple of hundred dollars off your asking price, but stay well above your expected price.

Always bite your tongue and let them react to your counteroffer before you say another word.

If they react negatively, ask them what they'd be willing to pay. If that's ridiculously low, reject it politely and thank them for coming, adding that it's clear they aren't that enthusiastic about the car and you're sure someone else will be. If their willing-to-pay number is not that bad but still below your expected price, counter with that price.

Somewhere in this kind of firm-but-flexible exchange, you'll get a price you'll find acceptable, one that's a lot better than any car store will give you.

A NOTE OF CAUTION

Unfortunately, we live in a hazardous world. One of the risks you face in selling your car yourself is that it could be *stolen* by a prospective "buyer" during a test drive. The thief may even leave another stolen car with you. (He may be trading up.)

Here are some thoughts on handling this potentially delicate situation:

- Don't let anyone test-drive your car unaccompanied.

- But be wary. You wouldn't get into a stranger's car alone, so why get into your car alone with a stranger? Have a friend accompany you.

- It's perfectly proper to ask a stranger for identification before permitting a test drive. Check a driver's license and a credit card, and leave those items with a friend or neighbor until you return. If the potential buyer carries no identification or won't cooperate, tell him that you're sorry but you won't allow anyone to test-drive your car without seeing and retaining proper identification.

- Trust your instincts. If you've got any reservations about a person, politely decline the request for a test drive.

- Some serious buyers will want to have your car checked over by a mechanic—an inspection they will pay for. That's a reasonable request, and a sign that you've got an excellent prospect. Again, however, you must be wary. You need a security deposit important enough to guarantee their return—perhaps a wallet full of important identification papers and credit cards. Alternatively, you might retain their current car and keys, after checking the registration information against their other identification data.

Some prospects may be offended by your caution, but if you ask them to put themselves in your place most will say they'd handle the situation the same way.

TIE UP THE LOOSE ENDS NEATLY

In closing the deal, be sure to do these important things:

- Get a nonrefundable deposit in return for taking the car off the market.

- Ask the buyer to get a certified check made out to you for the full sales price and to meet you at your bank at a mutually convenient time to sign over the title. Don't give possession of the car until this is done.

- Write out a sales receipt, in duplicate, that says you've sold the car "as is" for the agreed amount, and include the buyer's name, address and driver's license number, plus the date and time of day and both signatures.

- Call your state's department of motor vehicles to learn how to release your liability for parking and/or traffic violations and civil litigation resulting from operation after the date of sale. Obtain and complete the required form, and mail it promptly.

- Inform your auto insurance agent that you no longer own the car. He will advise you whether to transfer, suspend or cancel your coverage.

We haven't tried to touch every base in this sell-it-yourself lesson. We've focused primarily on the money issues. If you have questions and need more counsel, you should call the financial institution that has your auto loan, your auto insurance agent, your state's motor vehicle department or your local auto club for more information. Now let's look at the issue of financing. (If you're paying cash, you can skip to Chapter 11.)

Let us all be happy and live within our means, even if we have to borrow the money to do it.
—Artemus Ward

10

Auto Financing 101

Always remember that everything that happens in a car store is designed to make money for that store. There's nothing wrong with that; it's our free enterprise system at work. And that same great system can work for you, too, if you take action at every step to keep it competitive. The first step is shopping for money, and the time to do it is before you visit any car stores.

DON'T GET REAR-ENDED

When you get down to negotiating a final deal, the salesman is going to want you to "buy" your financing money through his store. As indicated in Chapter 5, that's an important source of his store's profit on the back end of the transaction.

That's when another interested party will get involved—the F&I (finance and insurance) manager. There is a lot of pressure on him to add profit to every deal. He usually gets a commission on anything you buy on the back end, including financing and the life and disability insurance he'll try to include in the transaction. (Some F&I managers make more money than any salesman in the store.)

The dealership may arrange financing through a bank or finance company, or through the auto manufacturer's captive finance operation. These captives, such as Ford Motor Credit or General Motors Acceptance Corporation, are very important sources of credit. They provide about 40 percent of all new-car financing, roughly the same percentage accounted for by banks. The captives typically handle between 30 and 60 percent of the financing for their own vehicles. (GMAC is the largest finance company in the country, with more than $100 billion in assets.)

Understand, though, that no matter which company does the actual financing, the car store acts as a middleman and receives a commission or fee for its service. Most often, this income comes from a dealer finance reserve, which is the difference between the contract rate charged to the consumer and the retention rate earned by the bank or finance company.

As a rule of thumb, figure that a car store can *double* its gross profit on a sale if it arranges the financing. No wonder there's pressure there!

Depending on the deal with the lending institution, the car store's participation fee can amount to 5 percent or more of the loan. The longer the term and the higher the rate, the more interest you pay . . . and the more commission the car store receives.

Let's assume the dealer "buys" the money for an auto loan of $14,000 from a lending institution at 8.5 percent interest and "sells" it to you on a 48-month loan at 10.5 percent interest. Over a four-year period that little 2 percent spread will put a $645 profit in the dealer's pocket, nearly 5 percent of the loan amount.

SURPRISE: THE DEALER'S DEAL MAY BE A GOOD ONE

You may find that the financing available through the dealership is quite attractive. These days auto manufacturers are offering subsidized, lower-interest financing plans through their own finance companies to stimulate sales.

Some manufacturers also have "first-time buyer" financing programs to start building brand loyalty among a younger audience. The rates are typically higher than standard bank rates, but these programs are often geared to people who might not qualify for standard bank auto loans simply because they have little or no credit history.

So whether it's your first car or your twenty-first, the car store's current financing options are *always* worth checking out. *But doesn't common sense say that you should be able to buy money cheaper if there's no middleman's commission for the financing entity to pay?*

The only way to know whether the financing options the dealership presents are attractive is to shop competitively for money before you sit down in a negotiating session at any car store. Then, when you're in that session, you'll be able to compare the annualized percentage rates (APRs) charged under the different alternatives.

Unfortunately, many new-car buyers don't even bother to check out their financing options before entering the F&I manager's den. The Consumer Bankers Association reports that about 80 percent of a bank's new-auto loans are originated indirectly, at dealerships, whereas only 20 percent result from buyers visiting the bank themselves to prequalify for a loan before they purchase a vehicle.

As a result, every year hundreds of thousands of car buyers who could have qualified for direct auto loans at lower rates end up paying a lot more money *to the same banks,* with the difference going to the car stores. Welcome to America, folks—the land where the average consumer is more interested in the convenience of one-stop shopping than in smart money management. Fortunately, you are not going to fall into that trap.

SHOPPING FOR MONEY: A PRIMER

As a first step, you should decide the highest monthly payment you can handle comfortably, *including auto insurance.* Call your insurance agent and tell him what vehicles you're considering. He'll be glad to tell you what your insurance will cost. (He works on commission, too.) He may even influence your final choice if you find that one alternative costs much less to insure than another.

Then decide on a down payment. If part or all of this will come from the sale of your current car, go through the steps in Chapters 8 and 9 to learn what it's really worth under each of those scenarios.

CAUTION: DON'T DRIVE "UPSIDE DOWN"

As a general rule, we'd advise putting at least 20 percent down on any new vehicle and financing it over a maximum term of four years. If you can't handle those numbers without changing your lifestyle dramatically, you should buy a less expensive car. This advice may sound conservative, but it will help keep you from getting "upside down" when you want to sell or trade again.

You're "upside down" when the actual value of the vehicle is less than the principal you still owe on the loan. You've got negative equity in the car, and you'd literally have to pay someone to take it off your hands. Here's why it's easy to get "upside down" whenever you combine a small down payment with a long financing term (such as 10 percent down and a six-year loan):

• New cars are *terrible* investments. Knowledgeable people will tell you that, depending on the specific vehicle and the timing of your purchase, *most new cars or trucks depreciate from 15–20 percent to as much as 35–40 percent in the first few weeks you own them!* Only the most prestigious high-end luxury cars seem to hold their value significantly longer.

• Add the fact that your monthly payments will include more interest than principal until you get into the latter part of the payment schedule, and you can see how a car's value can go down much faster than your equity in it goes up. (This fact leaves you exposed to significant loss if your car is stolen or destroyed in an accident. Your insurance company will pay you the car's depreciated market value, but you may owe the bank or finance company much more. If you are unwilling to accept this risk, ask the lender about gap insurance, which covers the difference between the car's insured value and the amount you owe. This insurance could cost several hundred dollars over the term of the loan.)

After you've decided whether to follow our 20 percent down/four-year rule or some other payment program, you're ready to contact some banks, your credit union and other new-car financing sources. (If you belong to a credit union, you should start there. Credit union rates on auto loans are typically at least one percent lower than bank rates. One reason: Credit unions usually don't provide a participation fee to car stores.)

☎ REACHING OUT AGAIN

Start this process on the telephone by calling a loan officer about car loans. Say that you're starting to shop for a new vehicle, that you want to line up financing first, that your credit report is clean, and that you'd like some help in finding the "price ball park" you should be shopping in. (We'll assume in the illustration below that you're following our 20 percent down, four-year guideline.)

First ask for their annualized percentage rates (APRs) on car loans. They will typically be higher for lower down payments and, sometimes, for longer payment schedules.

Tell the loan officer that you'd like to learn how large a loan you can afford if you put 20 percent down and finance a car over four years. Then take the total monthly payment you decided on, subtract one sixth of the semiannual auto insurance premium, and ask how large a four-year loan you could pay off with the remainder.

Add to that loan amount the down payment you decided on previously, and you'll have *the maximum price* you can afford to pay under those terms. (Remember, that total must cover state and local sales taxes, license and title fees, and any other up-front costs. Since license fees can be substantial, you should call your state's licensing agency and ask them to estimate the fee for a car in your price range.) Then, consider whether it's reasonable to expect to buy one or more of the vehicles you're interested in for that price or less, given what you'll learn in Chapter 14 about what they cost the dealer.

If your maximum affordable price is a lot lower than the dealer's invoice cost, and there's no current consumer rebate offer or factory-to-dealer incentive program, the answer is probably no. That means you've got to lower your sights to a less expensive vehicle, find more down-payment money, or ignore the 20 percent down/four-year rule and risk getting "upside down."

HERE'S SOMETHING THAT MIGHT HELP

Before you make that call, use the amortization table below to determine what the monthly payment would be for a given three-, four- or five-year loan.

As you can see, we've chosen annual percentage rates from 7.5 to 14, which should cover most of the realistic range. The dollar amounts in the table are the monthly payments per $1,000 borrowed. For example, assume you're borrowing $13,500 for four years at an annual percentage rate of 10.5. To calculate your monthly payment, go to the 10.5 percent column and find the payment per thousand for a four-year loan, $25.61. Multiplying that number by 13.5 (the number of thousands you're borrowing) gives you the monthly payment—$345.74

MONTHLY PAYMENTS FOR 3-, 4-, AND 5-YEAR LOANS

Payment Factors per $1,000	Annual Percentage Rates						
	7.5%	8.0%	8.5%	9.0%	9.5%	10.0%	10.5%
3-year loan	31.11	31.34	31.57	31.80	32.04	32.27	32.51
4-year loan	24.18	24.42	24.65	24.89	25.13	25.37	25.61
5-year loan	20.04	20.28	20.52	20.76	21.01	21.25	21.50
	11.0%	11.5%	12.0%	12.5%	13.0%	13.5%	14.0%
3-year loan	32.74	32.98	33.22	33.46	33.70	33.94	34.18
4-year loan	25.85	26.09	26.34	26.58	26.83	27.08	27.33
5-year loan	21.75	22.00	22.25	22.50	22.76	23.01	23.27

MAKING THEM COMPETE

You should shop for a money deal as aggressively as you're going to shop for that auto deal. Financial institutions are in a competitive business, too. (They only "book" about two thirds of the auto loans they approve.) Let them know you're shopping their competitors, and you'll borrow where you get the best terms.

It's worth the extra effort. Assume you borrow $15,000 on a four-year loan. If you could drop the interest rate just one percent by shopping competitively, you'd save over $300 in interest payments.

If your local bank quotes a rate higher than a bank five miles away, tell the loan officer you'd prefer to do business in your neighborhood but their rate is higher. Ask if that's absolutely the best they can do. She or he may have to get approval from another manager, but banks are in business to sell money and you may find there's room to negotiate. It's also common for a bank to give a slightly lower rate if you have an account there and the monthly payment is deducted automatically.

You can do a lot of comparison shopping on the telephone. In many cities you can even arrange your loan by telephone, calling in your application and getting an answer within a day or two.

Frequently, however, in-person meetings are advisable when you get down to two or three loan finalists, especially if you sense anything less than an enthusiastic response on the phone. Financial institutions want to build relationships with successful people, and being well-groomed and well-dressed can help create the right climate for loan approval.

Here are some more tips on financing:

1. Shop the dealers against the financial institutions

You should bargain aggressively to get the best interest rate from dealers. Usually, they have some flexibility. After reviewing your credit application, the automakers' captive finance companies often give dealers a range of interest rates they can charge you, with a low and a high number.

The best tactic is to make the dealer compete with your bank or credit union's best rate, and vice versa. Here's how one Fighting Chance customer reported on his experience: "I had a preapproved rate of 8.25 percent from a credit union. When the Chevy dealer's finance manager quoted 8.75 percent, I declined, stating the lower rate. He said he would match it. The next morning I called the credit union and told them I was going with GMAC. They said they would match GMAC or do better. I said I was tired of all the options, just give me your best rate. They gave me 7.85 percent, and GMAC could not match it."

2. Explore "the non-auto auto loan"

You may find, as *Fortune* has suggested in one of its investor's guides, that "a home equity credit line is a cheap, tax-smart way to buy a new car." That's because interest is tax-deductible on home equity borrowings up to $100,000, whereas other personal loan interest (including interest on standard auto loans) is not. The Consumer Bankers Association reports that nearly 10 percent of home equity loans are used to finance autos.

Home equity loans and lines of credit come in many forms, with either fixed or variable interest rates, and with and without "origination points." In most cases, you'll probably pay a lower *effective rate* than you would for a regular car loan, simply because the interest is deductible.

For example, if you're in the 31 percent tax bracket and the loan's annual percentage rate is 10.5, your net effective rate after taxes is only 7.25 percent. That may be significantly lower than any standard car loan rate you're likely to find. (We're not CPAs. You should check with your tax advisor for the best counsel.)

Incidentally, you will find *Money* magazine's monthly chart of "Leading Borrowing Deals" a useful source of information for both auto and home equity loans, with phone numbers to call for more information.

Another side to this that you should keep in mind is that with this type of financing, you'll be pledging *your home* as collateral. If there's any reason to be nervous about your ability to make those payments, you might sleep better with a standard auto loan, knowing that all they can repossess is your car, not your roof.

You should also note that Congress has become alarmed by a decline in the equity held by homeowners, caused in part by a sharp rise in tax-deductible home equity loans used for vacations and auto purchases. The lawmakers asked the General Accounting Office to investigate equity borrowing. After receiving the GAO's report, Congress may move to curb these tax advantages.

This makes it mandatory that you check with the appropriate tax counselor before proceeding.

3. Beware of the credit insurance rip-off

Don't get pressured into buying credit life insurance as an add-on. You'll often find this item buried in the mouse type in your auto loan documents. These policies are very profitable to both the insurance companies and the sellers—financial institutions and auto dealers who can earn commissions of 30 to 50 percent.

Money magazine reported that these policies pay out an average of only 38¢ in benefits for every dollar of premium, compared with 83¢ for the typical life insurance policy! And a spokesperson for the National Association of Insurance Commissioners has urged consumers to be particularly cautious of an insurer recommended by a *lender,* who is "going to be looking for the product with the highest commission, and that's usually the company that charges the highest premium."

By law, the purchase of credit life insurance cannot be a precondition for receiving a loan. Yet many people buy it. Ford Motor Credit Corporation reported that of the automobiles financed through a dealership, half of Ford's customers buy credit life insurance and 30 percent buy accident and health (disability) insurance. It's reasonable to project similar numbers for the other major auto manufacturers' captive credit operations.

If you feel you need any type of extra insurance coverage, discuss it with the agents you or your friends and relatives already deal with, and chances are you'll save a lot of money. Standard life and disability insurance policies are generally much better buys.

The bottom line: If you follow the steps we've suggested in this brief financing lesson, you'll be in a good position to determine whether the financing available at the car store is an attractive alternative for you or just a good deal for them.

A LITTLE TRAVELING MUSIC

We thought it would be appropriate to end this chapter with a song—one that F&I managers can sing to themselves on coffee breaks. So we've written these parody lyrics to the tune of that old standard, "Pennies from Heaven":

> Every time they finance here
> It's pennies from heaven.
> It's tough to keep my conscience clear
> With all these pennies from heaven.
> This really easy money just falls in my cup—
> You'd be amazed how quickly
> Those little pennies add up!
>
> All those banks and credit unions
> Think people are crazy.
> But we know one thing they don't—
> People are lazy!
> We give them one-stop shopping,
> They don't know that they pay.
> So there are pennies from heaven here every day!

11

The Fine Art

of Shopping

Without

Buying

A postal worker took his year-old car to a dealership in Providence, Rhode Island, for an oil change. To kill time while he was waiting, he browsed the showroom, admiring a fancy new sports car. Three salesmen converged on him.

Within minutes he found himself in the credit manager's office, loudly proclaiming that he wasn't in the market for anything new except oil. Before he knew it, he owned that sports car and a five-year payment schedule totaling $40,000.

He sued the dealership for engaging in deceptive trade practices. According to the Associated Press, his lawyer said, "I don't think he actually realized any paperwork had gone through. They made [him] feel empowered and enthusiastic about purchasing a new car. But the fact is [the dealership] took him for a ride and left him financially stranded."

W hile you're working on determining what your car is worth, deciding whether to sell it at wholesale or retail and getting your financial ducks in a row, you should also get to know some new cars well enough to narrow your choices to two or three finalists. You've been salivating over new-car ads for months. You know which models seem most appealing. Maybe you attended the annual automobile show when it came to town. You've devoured the model-year buyers' guides published by *Car and Driver* and *Road & Track,* which usually appear on supermarket shelves in late fall. You've studied the annual new-car issues of *Money* magazine, *Kiplinger's Personal Finance Magazine, Consumer Reports* and other sources for safety, economy, reliability and insurance cost ratings.

Even with all this information, narrowing your choices may not be easy. Domestic and foreign manufacturers typically offer 500 to 600 passenger car models for sale in the United States each model year!

The real challenge, however, isn't the number of cars; it's the number of car salesmen. You need a safe and secure way to get through the test-driving and information-gathering stage without getting caught up in the juggler's act. Here's how to accomplish that and live to tell about it.

First review Psychology 101 in Chapter 4 (pages 15–16), especially the part about projecting total emotional detachment. Then play the little game outlined next.

MAKE THIS AN AWAY GAME, IF YOU CAN

If you live in an area that has several dealers for each major make, gather your information at car stores that are relatively farther from your home or office. That way, when you're ready to start serious negotiations with stores closer to home or work, you'll be an unknown quantity, without the implied commitments of previous visits. (The less a salesman knows about you, the less money he'll get from you.)

That doesn't necessarily mean you should ignore those more distant stores in your final negotiations. Indeed, you may drive a better bargain with them because they'll see you as business they normally wouldn't get. They may agree to a lower gross deal just because you're an out-of-town bird in hand. But, as you'll learn in Chapter 19, there are real advantages to buying your new car from a dealer who's more convenient, ideally the one who'll service it regularly.

Plan these trips by checking the dealer association's advertising in your newspaper, where you'll probably find the names and addresses of all the dealers for a given make in your metropolitan area. You may even find a map showing their relative locations. (Dealers love to put maps in their ads!)

Choose the stores you'll visit, grab a pen and a pad to take detailed notes, *leave your checkbook and your credit cards at home,* and jump in your car.

Your objective on this trip is to narrow your choices to a few specific cars that will meet your requirements and make you a happy driver for the next several years. Smile, this is going to be fun!

THE GAME PLAN

As you enter the showroom, walk briskly to one of the younger-looking, less experienced salesmen. Tell him you're just starting to look at new cars, and yes, you do plan to buy one soon. But no, you're not a candidate to buy one today under any circumstances. There are several makes you want to research and test-drive before making a decision.

You have no idea what you'll end up buying. It'll depend on a lot of (unspecified) things. But he's got a couple of cars that are on your list, and you'd like to test-drive them, learn about their features and benefits, and get some literature to review at home.

While you're in this tire-kicking stage, test-drive at least two different cars you like at each dealership. Make those test drives long enough to put the cars through most of the paces you'll require of them every day. And be sure to drive cars equipped the way you think you'll buy them. (Don't test an automatic transmission if you want a stick shift or the four-door sedan if you want the coupe.)

Even if you love both cars, try not to show it. Remember that your behavior should say, A car is a car. I'm going to check them all out and buy the best deal.

When you're around that salesman, act undecided, uncommitted, even a little wishy-washy. For each car, comment on things you like and things you don't like. (If you like everything, invent a few things you don't like.) That will keep him from moving into his aggressive selling posture with the "if" questions designed to get verbal commitments, such as "If I got you the right price, would you buy this car today?" When he asks that, your correct answer is, "Not today. As I told you, I'm just starting to narrow my choices. I've got more appointments to test-drive cars today and tomorrow, and I plan to keep them."

ANYTHING YOU SAY WILL BE USED AGAINST YOU

Remember, the one who asks the questions controls the conversation. So ask him all the things you need to know, such as "What rustproofing warranty comes with the car?" And "What specific direct consumer incentives is the factory offering this month on the cars you sell?" And one he probably won't answer in detail, "What specific factory-to-dealer cash incentives are in effect this month?"

But when he asks you questions, your stock answers should be, "I don't know," "I'm not sure," "I need to discuss it with my spouse," and "I'll have to think about that." When those get tired, answer a question with a question—for example, "How do most people answer that?"

In this little game, you'll get the information you need, but he'll get nothing concrete to move toward his objective of closing you before you leave. (Remember, he's in a sell-it-now-or-never business, but you're in a don't-buy-it-now mode.)

After test-driving cars you particularly like, write down the key information from the *manufacturer's* window sticker (not the dealer's separate sticker): the vehicle identification number, model number and suggested retail price for the base car, plus the contents and prices of the optional factory equipment packages and other accessories.

Then thank the salesman for his time. Take his card, but don't give him your phone number or address. If he discovers that you live two gas stops from his store, he'll decide that it's now or never and try to chain you to a chair until you buy.

Above all, don't get roped into his office to talk about anything, including the weather. He's going to want you to sit down for a minute "just to see what it looks like on paper." Tell him politely that you're not ready to do that, and that you've got appointments to test-drive three other makes. Both statements will be true.

If you live in a smaller market without many dealers for the same make, you can't play the game exactly like this. But the essential rule still applies: *You want to get all the information you need while giving him none of the information he needs.*

NARROW THE FIELD, BUT NOT TOO MUCH

After a day or two, you should be able to narrow your choices to a few favorites. Try to keep at least two or three in the running. The big winners in this game will be those who maintain several options right down to the finish line. A single choice isn't an option, it's an obsession—one that's potentially very expensive.

SHAKE THE FAMILY TREE

One good way to open options is to consider "family relations," vehicles that have different brand names but are made by the same manufacturer and are quite similar. The key differences often will be in trim levels, but there also can be meaningful price differences.

For example, Chrysler's midsize sedans, the Dodge Intrepid, Eagle Vision and Chrysler Concorde, are essentially similar vehicles at different price points. Ditto for the Ford Taurus and the Mercury Sable, the Chevy Blazer and the GMC Jimmy, etc.

At any time, there could also be hefty manufacturer incentives offered on some family members but not on others.

If you like one branch of a family tree you may like another almost as well. And pricing and incentive differences may be meaningful enough to swing your choice to a vehicle you hadn't considered at the start.

Here is a list of "family relations," some of which are the products of joint ventures between automotive manufacturers (e.g., Ford and Mazda):

"FAMILY RELATIONS"

General Motors:

- Buick Century & Oldsmobile Cutlass Ciera/Cruiser
- Buick LeSabre, Oldsmobile Eighty-Eight Royale & Pontiac Bonneville
- Buick Park Avenue & Oldsmobile Ninety-Eight
- Buick Regal, Chevrolet Lumina, Oldsmobile Cutlass Supreme & Pontiac Grand Prix
- Buick Roadmaster & Chevrolet Caprice
- Buick Skylark, Oldsmobile Achieva & Pontiac Grand Am
- Cadillac Seville (4-door) & Cadillac Eldorado (2-door)
- Chevrolet Astro & GMC Safari
- Chevrolet Beretta (2-door) & Chevrolet Corsica (4-door)
- Chevrolet Tahoe & GMC Yukon
- Chevrolet Blazer, GMC Jimmy & Oldsmobile Bravada
- Chevrolet Camaro & Pontiac Firebird
- Chevrolet Cavalier & Pontiac Sunfire
- Chevrolet Lumina, Oldsmobile Silhouette & Pontiac Trans Sport minivans
- Chevrolet S-Series Pickup & GMC Sonoma Pickup

- Chevrolet Full-Size Pickups & GMC Sierra Pickups
- Chevrolet Sportvan & GMC Rally
- Chevrolet Suburban & GMC Suburban

Chrysler (and partner Mitsubishi):

- Chrysler Concorde, Dodge Intrepid & Eagle Vision
- Chrysler LHS & Chrysler New Yorker
- Dodge Caravan & Plymouth Voyager minivans
- Dodge Grand Caravan, Chrysler Town & Country & Plymouth Grand Voyager minivans
- Dodge Neon & Plymouth Neon
- Dodge Stealth & Mitsubishi 3000GT
- Eagle Summit & Mitsubishi Mirage
- Eagle Talon & Mitsubishi Eclipse

Ford (and partners Mazda & Nissan):

- Ford Contour & Mercury Mystique
- Ford Crown Victoria & Mercury Grand Marquis
- Ford Escort & Mercury Tracer
- Ford Probe & Mazda MX-6
- Ford Taurus & Mercury Sable
- Ford Thunderbird & Mercury Cougar
- Mercury Villager & Nissan Quest minivans

Others:

- Geo Metro & Suzuki Swift
- Geo Prizm & Toyota Corolla
- Geo Tracker & Suzuki Sidekick
- Nissan Maxima & Infiniti I30
- Toyota Camry V6 XLE & Lexus ES 300

CONSIDER THE BIG HIDDEN COST: DEPRECIATION

As you're assessing alternatives, remember that the most significant cost of car ownership isn't gas or maintenance or repairs or insurance. It's depreciation— the difference between what you pay to acquire it and what you'll get when you sell it as it moves down the automotive feeding chain. Some cars retain their value better than others, and you should factor these differences into your thinking.

Here's an example. Ford's Taurus and Honda's Accord are family sedans in the same general price range. Yet the Automotive Lease Guide's residual value tables consistently show that the wholesale value of a two-year-old Taurus LX sedan will be about 50 percent of its original sticker price (MSRP), whereas a two-year-old Accord LX will command about 60 percent of its sticker. Thus, if you negotiated the same price for each, you'd save about $100 a month over two years by choosing the Honda. (To check projected depreciation for the vehicles you're considering, you may purchase the latest bimonthly issue of the Automotive Lease Guide's *Residual Percentage Guide* from Chart Software; 800-418-8450.)

COMPARE THE WARRANTIES

If several vehicles appeal to your eye, some may look better than others after you compare their basic bumper-to-bumper warranties. The industry standard is 36/36,000, which means that most parts of the car are covered for manufacturer's defects for 36 months or 36,000 miles, whichever comes first. (Typically, the battery and tires are not covered by the basic warranty.)

If you check the warranty table in Chapter 18, you'll note that some automakers offer better basic coverage than others. As an example, assume that you like the Honda Passport and its cousin, the Isuzu Rodeo, equally well. Honda's basic warranty is 36/36,000, but Isuzu's is 36/50,000. If you drive substantially more than 12,000 miles a year, that difference may tip the scales in Isuzu's favor.

CHECK THE COST OF REGULAR MAINTENANCE

Every new vehicle comes with a booklet which outlines the maintenance schedule recommended by the manufacturer. The booklet is free, but the service is expensive. (New car dealers make most of their profits from parts and service, and that little booklet is a major source of their continuing prosperity, whether car sales are up or down.) As with insurance premiums, the cost of regularly scheduled maintenance can differ from one vehicle to another.

To get a handle on this, call the local dealerships for the models you're considering and ask to speak to a service advisor. (This is the person who meets customers as they drive in and writes up each service order.) Make this call in mid-afternoon, when most of his contact and follow-up with today's customers are behind him. Tell him which car you're considering buying, and say you're interested in learning about the costs of recommended maintenance. Inquire about the mileage intervals for regular service in the first two years, and ask him to tell you the approximate costs for each visit.

IF YOU'VE GOT A QUESTION, CALL HOME

If you can't get all your important questions answered by people at a dealership, try calling the manufacturer. You'll find a list of their phone numbers in the Appendix.

THE SMART SHOPPER'S TIEBREAKER

If you're having difficulty choosing a favorite, here's an idea that beats flipping a coin: Consider *renting* each finalist for a day or so on weekends, as a way to learn more than you can in those brief test drives. This will set you back a few dollars, but the rental cost pales in comparison to the financial and emotional cost of buying the wrong car.

You may have to make several calls to find what you want, but most popular domestic and import models can be rented. In fact, many dealers rent cars by the day.

However you narrow the field, remember to retain one or two fallback choices. At this stage, throwing away alternatives is throwing away leverage.

Saturn:

A Different

Kind of Deal

Now, they finally have a car do what GM said it would do—compete on a quality basis with small Japanese cars, specifically the Honda Civic—and the most creative thing they can come up with is a no-haggle pricing policy that, while supposedly for the benefit of the consumer, is really just another price hike in disguise.

—From a consumer's letter written in response to a *Business Week* cover story on Saturn

The folksy, down-home ad campaign for GM's Saturn subsidiary carries the tag line, "A Different Kind of Company. A Different Kind of Car." They could add, "A Different Kind of Deal."

There's apparently a lot to like in Saturn, General Motors' version of a Japanese subcompact. It's earned high customer satisfaction ratings in the

J. D. Power and Associates Initial Quality Studies[sm]. *Car and Driver* called it "the luxury econocar, tightly built and brimming with niceties."

Designed as an import fighter, it's doing its job well; about half of Saturn's customers would have opted for an import instead. And seven out of ten sales have been to those who would not otherwise have bought a GM product.

But the biggest difference between Saturn and the rest of the auto industry isn't in the car, it's in the deal. *There isn't any.* If you want a Saturn, you'll pay the full sticker price, even if the sales manager is your brother-in-law. The reason: *There's no competition between dealers for your business. And there isn't going to be any.*

THE KEY: ELIMINATING COMPETITIVE GEOGRAPHY

Starting with a clean sheet of paper, Saturn was able to give each dealer a large, exclusive sales territory. Each market area has only one retail "owner," which effectively eliminates price competition between dealers. This exclusive selling territory could be one part of a huge market, like Los Angeles, or the entire metropolitan area of a smaller market, such as San Diego. In effect, GM has taken one of the most competitive retail businesses and made it noncompetitive for this brand.

With no other Saturn dealers within a reasonable shopping radius, you won't be able to play one dealer off against another to negotiate price. Although GM will say that a dealership may charge what it wishes, the cold, hard fact is that the sticker price is the real price. *Think of it as a legal form of retail price-fixing.*

It's also Saturn's policy not to offer rebates or other incentives—which saves GM anywhere from $500 to $1,500 per vehicle, depending on the competitive climate.

The bottom line for consumers: They will pay at least $1,000 more for a Saturn than they would if Saturn had been, say, just another Chevrolet model instead of a separate GM division with an exclusive-territory dealer network. And the normal market forces of supply and demand will have no impact on pricing.

The bottom line for dealers: They make a lot more money under this exclusive-territory pricing umbrella. With guaranteed front-end gross profits per sale up to $1,700 or more, Saturn is the most profitable small-car franchise by a country mile. Plenty of large-car franchises would gladly trade bottom lines with any Saturn store.

HAVING THEIR CAKE AND EATING IT: A PSYCHOLOGICAL COUP

Fixed pricing doesn't seem to hurt sales: Saturn routinely sells more vehicles per dealer than any other auto franchise, including Ford, Chevy and Toyota (which sell both cars and trucks). In most years, dealers are selling every car the factory can make.

Ironically, Saturn's "no-dicker" sticker is a key ingredient in its success because it eliminates the haggling over price. In the showroom, for a refreshing change, Saturn customers are treated like a bona fide form of intelligent life. The salespeople simply help them fall in love with the car, tell them that the sticker price is fair and (most importantly) assure them no one will get the car for less. No sales pressure is applied.

In grateful response, Saturn buyers pay more than they would for comparable small cars sold by dealers willing to negotiate and factories willing to use incentives. Most of them don't have a clue that the dealer's profit on their purchase is much greater than he could realize with any other small-car franchise in America. They're so focused on the new-and-improved purchase process that they actually enjoy paying more.

The halo of this more pleasant shopping experience carries over to enhance their ratings of the vehicle itself. (Isn't a diner more likely to praise the food when the chef has been a superb host?) These ratings, in turn, enhance Saturn's used-car value as it moves down the automotive feeding chain. Its resale value has been above that of most domestic makes and comparable to the best of the Japanese competitors.

The financial picture isn't nearly as rosy for General Motors. The company spent about $5 billion to launch Saturn, and it's not clear whether the stockholders will ever see an adequate return on that investment. Small cars don't produce big profits per unit. Saturn's production capacity is limited, and the capital infusions requested by other needy GM divisions may represent more critical corporate priorities than expanding Saturn.

Saturn's product line will change over the years, but the prognosis for prospective customers is "more of the same": More profit for dealers because of exclusive sales territories. Perhaps more aggressive price increases than for other domestic cars. And no deals for anyone.

WHAT'S A SHOPPER TO DO?

You've got two choices:

1. *If your heart's set on a Saturn, relax and enjoy it; it's a great little car, and you're striking a blow for U.S. economic resurgence.* Instead of haggling over price, you'll be treated like visiting royalty. And why shouldn't you be? You're paying the sticker price!

(Think about it for ten seconds. If you called any dealer in the United States and told him you were on your way down to pay the sticker price for one of his cars, he'd probably send a limousine to pick you up, if only to keep you from stopping at another car store on the way. At that price, you'd have a wonderful sales experience anywhere.)

The Saturn dealer might make three times the profit on your purchase that he's making selling more expensive cars in his non-Saturn stores. But you'll have the consolation of knowing that the next customer will make a similar contribution to his welfare. No one will walk in and get the car you bought for $1,000 less. It seems almost un-American, doesn't it?

Here's choice number two:

2. *If Saturn is only one of your finalists, you should shop the competition aggressively.* (That includes the Toyota Corolla and Geo Prizm, Ford Escort, Nissan Sentra, Honda Civic, Toyota Tercel and the Dodge and Plymouth Neons.) Saturn accounts for less than one of every twenty passenger cars sold. You may like some of the other nineteen better, and you shouldn't have to pay the sticker price for any of them.

Facing more flexible dealers and frequent factory incentive programs, you may even discover that you can afford a higher trim level in another car for the price of Saturn's lower-level offering. As one reader wrote in response to *Car and Driver*'s comparison of several subcompacts: "Except for the Saturn, all the cars in your comparison could be purchased for well below the sticker price, including sound system and air conditioning. Only Saturn dealers refuse to dicker. The real competitors in the Saturn's price range are the four-door upscale models of the cars you tested. Saturn offers good value, but in the real world it is not necessarily the best buy."

Warning: We have heard that Saturn dealers don't exactly lead the league when it comes to trade-in allowances for your used car. Many customers relax their guard in that no-pressure sales situation and end up accepting low-ball offers. Don't let that happen to you. Reread Chapter 8, and be sure you know the true wholesale value of your current car before you enter Saturn's seductive web.

Saturn is a different kind of company. Exclusive sales areas are a terrific idea for both the company and its dealers. But if all automotive franchises were set up that way, U.S. consumers would spend billions of dollars more on basic transportation every year.

A LITTLE MORE TRAVELING MUSIC

We think Saturn needs a company song, one the dealers can sing to celebrate their good fortune at annual sales conventions. So we've written one called "You Gotta Be a Saturn Dealer," to be sung to the tune of "You Gotta Be a Football Hero," a song you may have heard your father sing. We thought it would be appropriate to end this chapter with the lyrics.

> You gotta be a Saturn dealer
> To make the max when you sell 'em a car.
> You gotta have exclusive rights to the town
> 'Cause that guarantees the price can't come down.
> To find another Saturn dealer
> They'll have to drive to Timbuktu.
> You gotta be a Saturn dealer
> To see what's really in this business for you!
>
> You gotta be a Saturn dealer
> To sell this great new American car.
> There's lots of other great little cars,
> There's only one hitch—they can't make you this rich!
> So save your tears for General Motors,
> They're five billion bucks in the tank.
> But they made me a Saturn dealer
> So I'm cryin' all the way to the bank!
> (They pay the sticker)
> I'm cryin' all the way to the bank!
> (So will my mother)
> I'm cryin' all the way to the bank!

13

One-Price, "No-Dicker" Dealers: Oasis or Mirage?

Before its initial sales year ended, it had become clear to the automotive establishment that Saturn's greatest achievement was getting American car buyers to pay the sticker price for every car, and that the key to pulling off this startling coup was the elimination of haggling over price. Success in any field breeds imitation.

THE SATURN WANNABES

Other dealers, watching Saturn's apparently magical scenario unfold, decided to play follow-the-leader. They had seen the new religion, and they were converting—dumping their high-pressure sales forces and becoming one-price, "no-dicker" dealers.

That "fair" price would be somewhere between the sticker price and the dealer invoice price. It would be noted on a separate "civilized sticker" placed on each car, and there would be no bargaining. What you see is what you pay. For everyone.

Depending on the current popularity of this selling technique, the number of "no-dicker" dealers ranges from a few hundred to over 1,000—a small fraction of the 22,000+ franchised dealerships. Some make the switch in desperation when sales are so poor they have nothing to lose. Others simply think it's a good idea and want to reap the benefits of getting there first in their markets.

Eventually, most of them realize they've got a problem they can't solve: Without exclusive sales territories, they don't have Saturn's fail-safe formula working for them. It's like grafting an eagle's wings onto a pigeon; that pigeon can soar, but without talons it can't catch fish.

Let's examine how this pricing transplant works, from both consumer and dealer perspectives.

FOR THE SHOPPER, THERE'S LESS THERE THAN MEETS THE EYE

How do these "no-dicker" dealerships operate, from the buyer's perspective? J. D. Power and Associates conducted a study of twenty-four dealerships that had adopted the system relatively early. The findings, widely reported by the Associated Press, revealed the following:

1. *"No-dicker" dealers make more profit.* (Otherwise, why do it?) Nine out of ten dealers reported increased sales since adopting the program. And half the dealers said their average gross profit per car had gone up; the other half split equally between those whose profits were the same and those with lower profits per sale.

Overall, the "no-dicker" system seemed to be doing what it was designed to do: get the consumer to pay more for new vehicles.

2. *Today's price is just that; tomorrow's price is anybody's guess.* If consumers expect to have a Saturn-like experience at other "no-dicker" dealers, leaving confident that no one will buy the same car for a lower price next week, or tomorrow, they're in for a surprise.

- The research showed that 33 percent of these dealers changed their "civilized" prices as factory incentive programs changed (a frequent occurrence).
- Another 29 percent of the dealers changed prices as their inventory conditions changed (another frequent occurrence).
- And 14 percent of dealers changed prices "when they needed to boost volume," another 14 percent changed them weekly, and 10 percent changed them every two or three days!

So buyers may have a more enjoyable shopping experience, but they will pay more for the car, and someone else may pay a lot less for the same vehicle tomorrow. And in most cases, they'll still have to dicker over their trade-in allowance and deal with the F&I manager on financing and back-end options.

Does that sound like what you expected, or hoped for, when you heard about one-price, "no-dicker" dealers? (We don't think so.)

BEWARE OF CAR SALESMEN BEARING DOUGHNUTS

Just as cigarette packages carry mandatory warnings, some one-price stores should be required to post "Buyer Beware" signs. Shopping incognito with a newspaper reporter, we walked into a big "no-dicker" Ford dealership, where there was coffee and doughnuts and absolutely no pressure. The salesman just walked us around the lot, where the price of every car was on the windshield. He said business was up 42 percent since the store switched to one-price selling—an amazing statistic, considering that this had to be one of the highest-priced Ford stores in the state. Their price on a mid-line Taurus was one the village idiot could have beaten by at least $1,000 with one phone call to any other Ford store in the city. Yet business was up 42 percent!

Now, everybody wants to go to heaven, yet nobody wants to die. But wouldn't you think that one or two of those customers, waking up in heaven, might want to check for their names in the obituary column? They were lulled into lowering their guard by a "we're-on-your-side" selling approach that set them up for the big tumble, which they never even felt. One more triumph for American marketing ingenuity.

To avoid becoming the next victim, remember Bragg's Golden Rule:

Whether it's Saturn or one of these Saturn wannabes, assume that the more pleasant the purchase experience, the more gold is being lifted from your wallet. Sadly, it's often true that the lower the pressure, the higher the price.

FOR THE DEALER, "NO-DICKER" IS NO NIRVANA

Without the Saturn-like umbrella of exclusive sales territories, "no-dicker" dealers are trying to light a match in a deluge. Here's why you won't see this selling policy adopted broadly:

- In most large markets there are several dealers for the same make. (Chevrolet and Ford, for example, each have over 4,000 dealers nationally.) When one adopts a "no-dicker" policy, he becomes a sitting duck for the others, who can cut prices selectively to steal his customers.

- The 80/20 Rule of Life still applies. Many dealers will be reluctant to give up their shot at the least knowledgeable 20 percent of the buyers, the ones who probably provide 80 percent of the profits.

- In effect, one-price selling says to the customer, "Pay it or go somewhere else." That's not a message most dealers want to deliver. They'd rather make a small profit than lose the sale to a competitor.

- "No-dicker" is a better strategy for tough times, when sales are hardest to come by. When consumer confidence and sales traffic are strong, "no-dicker" makes less economic sense to dealers.

As a spokesperson for the National Automobile Dealers Association said in response to questions about the "no-dicker" movement, "Dealers sell the way they do because it works. They are real wizards at local marketing, and they do what works."

- Finally, and most important, the bulk of dealers can't change to "no-dicker" successfully unless the customer changes, too. But the customer has been trained under the current system, the one dealers use "because it works."

What are the chances of most shoppers buying a car at the first price offered? Slim, indeed. After decades of 20,000 dealers shouting "Shop us last" in their advertising, the cumulative impact has taught consumers that there will always be a better price down the street. As a result, research consistently shows that most new-car buyers prefer to negotiate prices.

As a former mega-dealer in Los Angeles said before he closed his last store, "People will shop you silly, and they should, too...sooner or later, someone will sell you a car for the price you want."

The retail auto dealers of America forced the customer's genie out of the bottle a long time ago, and they can't put him back with "no-dicker" stickers. Until the other automotive franchises find a way to reinvent their distribution channels, providing exclusive sales territories for a smaller number of dealers, Saturn will be the only make that can enforce this policy consistently.

Long-term, the market is going to set the price. Supply and demand: It's the law.

FOR SMART SHOPPERS, THE "NO-DICKER" DEALER IS A USEFUL TOOL

Use him! If the "no-dicker" price is friendly enough, buy from him. If it's not, use it as a place to start negotiating with other dealers. To win your business, they'll have to beat it, maybe by a lot.

DON'T CONFUSE A MANUFACTURER'S "VALUE-PRICING" OFFERINGS WITH "NO-DICKER" DEALERS

There's another, related pricing practice. It's usually called "value pricing," and it's used most often by General Motors (and to a lesser extent by Ford). Typically, the company will package certain models with a standard list of popular options and offer them for an attractively low price.

There are two things you should understand about value pricing:

• You won't often find it on the exciting new models. Value-priced cars are almost always models that badly need updating. General Motors' goal is to replace its models every four or five years, as the Japanese do. But that doesn't always happen, and it's hard to get today's prices for yesterday's sheet metal. In that scenario, GM's big idea is value pricing. It's a tactic that can help for a while, but in the new-car business you eventually have to offer the consumer cars that are truly new.

• Value pricing usually contains a healthy dose of smoke-and-mirrors. That's because the automakers achieve a big part of the retail price "reduction" simply by cutting the dealer's gross profit margin. Recognizing that most buyers don't pay the sticker price, they reduce the MSRP to a number that's closer to a realistic transaction price. As an example, if the old pricing provided a $2,500 spread between the dealer invoice price and the MSRP, value pricing might reduce the built-in profit to $1,000. *Is that a real price reduction?* Of course not, because the MSRP wasn't a real price in the first place. (If you subtract thin air from thin air, you don't save any real dollars.)

The manufacturers and their dealers would like to sell these cars on a one-price, "no-dicker" basis. They won't, because most domestic makes have thousands of dealers competing with each other. As Ford's general manager said, "We can suggest a price, but if the market won't bring it, the dealers are going to cut into their gross to make the deal." Also, it's not unusual to find manufacturers offering incentives on value-priced cars that are selling poorly.

These specially equipped and priced vehicles can be great buys. And if you shop around, you're likely to find some price flexibility, too. Our advice: If you live in or near a major market, don't pay the MSRP for any value-priced car, because there will be another dealer who will sell the car for less.

It happened at a convention of the National Automobile Dealers Association in Dallas. The president of Chevrolet's Dealer Council got up and asked his cohorts to sell one more Chevy a week, even if they made no profit on it.

Why? Because that would mean another 250,000 Chevys sold each year, giving GM billions more for new product programs over the next few years. (And you thought those guys had no heart.)

The lesson: Learn what those cars really cost the dealer. Because, yes, you can buy them for cost, or very close to it.

Learn

the Cost

or Pay

the Price

Of all the insights we've gained from Fighting Chance customers, this is the most important: *Most dealers agree to several slim-profit deals each month with customers who have done their homework and know how to use it.*

What's a slim-profit deal? For a popular mid-priced family sedan, just a few hundred dollars over the dealer invoice price, not counting incentives (which would reduce the price further). For a high-end luxury import, from $1,500 to $3,000 over invoice.

Why do dealers who make a killing with some customers agree to slim-profit deals with others? For four key reasons:

- First and foremost, they're in a sales-driven, ego-driven business. At the end of each month, the first question anyone asks is *how many cars did we sell,* not *how much profit did we make on each deal.* By definition, almost any sale is a good sale.

- Frequently, a dealer's future supply is based on his current sales performance. It's called "turn and earn." Most dealers are terminal optimists, and they want to be sure their vehicle allocation will always be sufficient to support their dreams. In this business, an extra sale today means an extra sale tomorrow.

- Once they understand that you're a knowledgeable shopper who will negotiate a slim-profit deal, they'd rather take the slim profit than give the sale to a competitor. Selling one more car this month and making a modest profit always beats not selling it and making no profit.

- Finally, since they make the bulk of their profits from parts and service, they want their sold vehicles out on the road, where they will generate a steady income stream.

The centerpiece of your ability to negotiate a slim-profit deal will be your knowledge of what that car or truck is going to cost the dealer. With that information, you'll know whether the deal is a good or bad one before you agree to it. That, of course, is the last thing the dealer wants you to know. He wants his salesmen to negotiate based on the sticker price, not the cost.

Frequently, after we make this point on a radio talk show, the first caller is an irate dealer who says "What right has anyone got to know what I pay for the products I sell? You don't know what a retailer pays for a TV set or anything else you buy." Our response is always the same: "Yes, but you don't get home with your new TV and learn that your neighbor paid $100 less for the same set because he knew something you didn't know. As long as you auto dealers have a selling system geared to take advantage of uninformed people, the public has a right to public information to protect itself." End of debate.

IT'S A THREE-PIECE PUZZLE

Three key elements determine the dealer cost of any vehicle:

1. Dealer Invoice Price—the actual factory invoice billed to the dealer.

2. Factory-to-Dealer Incentives—cash paid only to dealers, details of which are not widely publicized to consumers.

3. Dealer Holdback—a portion of the factory invoice price which is collected and "held back" by the manufacturer, then refunded periodically to the dealer as the vehicles are sold. Holdback has been used for decades by General Motors, Ford and Chrysler. In recent years, almost all imports have adopted the concept. Today, holdback applies to nine of every ten vehicles sold in the United States.

Without learning about all three elements, you can't get a good fix on what the dealer pays for a given vehicle. Let's tackle them one at a time.

THE STARTING POINT: DEALER INVOICE PRICE

This is the actual price billed by the factory, the invoice the dealer must pay when the vehicle is delivered to his lot. (Typically, the dealer pays the manufacturer with money he borrows under his "flooring plan" credit arrangement with a bank or finance company or with the auto manufacturer's finance subsidiary. He pays the lender interest until the car is sold, then repays the loan.)

To determine this figure, you need a printout of dealer invoice prices for the specific vehicle or vehicles you're considering. To get familiar with the kind of information contained on a printout, turn to pages 178–179 of the Appendix and look at the simplified pricing data we've created for a fictitious car and manufacturer—the All-American Speedster, built by the All-American Motor Corporation.

Our simplified printout for the All-American Speedster contains the following information:

• You will find both the Dealer Invoice Price and the Manufacturer's Suggested Retail Price (MSRP), which is the price you'll see on the sticker attached to the window of each new car or truck. Note that the list shows pricing for all available body styles and trim levels, from the least expensive low-end Speedster model to the most expensive high-end model.

• Just below the initial price table you will find a complete listing of all the standard equipment items that are included in the base price of each trim level.

- You will then see dealer invoice and retail price information for all available factory-installed optional equipment and accessories, including those sold as packages and groups.

- The Factory Code column on the far left carries the actual manufacturer's computer code, the number by which each model or accessory is ordered or identified, just as it appears on the window sticker of a new car or truck.

It's important to have a printout covering all the configurations a manufacturer offers for a given vehicle. Without the complete picture, you can't make price/value comparisons between different trim levels. (For example, a higher trim level frequently represents a better value because it includes standard equipment in the base price that would be treated as extra-cost options in a lower trim level.)

Building Your Worksheet

Once you have current pricing printouts for the vehicles you're interested in, you can determine the dealer invoice cost for the specific models you want, outfitted with the exact optional accessories and equipment you choose. To illustrate how easy this is, we'll build a simple worksheet using the pricing data we've created for our fictitious car—the All-American Speedster.

- Let's assume you're interested in a Speedster wagon. You don't want the lowest trim level (A), but you can't justify spending an extra $3,000+ for the highest trim level (AAA) because you really don't need things like luxury cloth upholstery and a tachometer. So you settle on the middle trim level (AA, Factory Code S87), with a sticker price of $15,200 and a dealer invoice price of $13,000. Note that we have entered these numbers on the New-Vehicle Worksheet on page 69.

- Looking at the Preferred Equipment Packages available for the AA wagon, you're attracted by Factory Code 444B, which includes air conditioning, rear window defroster, AM/FM stereo radio w/cassette, power door locks, power windows and cruise control. The package price is less than what the items would cost separately. The retail price is $1,800; the dealer invoice price, $1,500. We have added these numbers to the worksheet on page 69.

- You'd also like to have a more powerful engine than the standard 3.0-liter V6. Looking at the Equipment and Accessories list, you see that you can add a 3.8-liter V6 (Factory Code 947). Sticker price: $560; invoice: $470. These numbers are also placed on the worksheet.

NEW-VEHICLE WORKSHEET

Factory Code #	Model & Optional Equipment	Dealer Invoice Price	Suggested Retail Price
S87	All-American Speedster AA 4-Door Wagon	$13,000	$15,200
444B	Preferred Equipment Package	1,500	1,800
	(air conditioner, rear window defroster, power door locks, power driver seat, power windows, cruise control, AM/FM/cassette, P205/65R15 SBR blackwall tires)		
947	3.8-liter V6 engine upgrade	470	560
314	Rear-facing third seat	130	160
	Subtotals	15,100	17,720
	Plus Destination Charges	500	500
	Subtotals	15,600	18,220
	Less: Direct Consumer Rebate (coming up next)	750	
	Less: Factory-to-Dealer Incentives (also coming up next)	200	
	Less: Dealer Holdback (to be discussed after that)	532	
	Subtotals	14,118	18,220
	Less: Assumed Year-End Carryover Allowance (After new models are introduced. Covered in Chapter 15.)	911	
	Grand Totals	$13,207	$18,220

- The only other item you want is a rear-facing third seat (Factory Code 314). This adds $130 invoice, $160 retail to our worksheet.

- We must also add the $500 destination (freight) charge. Note that there is no markup on freight; the dealer simply charges the buyer what the manufacturer charges him. Note also that the sticker price does not include sales taxes or license and title fees.

- Adding the subtotals in the two columns, we find that there's a difference of $2,620 between the suggested retail price ($18,220) and the dealer invoice price ($15,600). This difference is a starting point for understanding the dealer's real cost, but it's not the whole story, as the last few lines of the worksheet imply. We'll return to those lines later in this chapter.

We'll discuss in Chapter 20 exactly how to use this dealer invoice cost information in the negotiation process. For now, let's just say that the $2,620 difference between the dealer's cost and the retail price allows significant room for price movement, in your direction.

Pricing Credentials You Can Count On

At some point in the shopping process, a salesman is likely to tell you that your information on dealer invoice pricing is wrong. If you received your pricing data from us, you may confidently invite him to take out the vehicle's actual invoice for a comparison.

The reason you can be confident in the numbers is at the bottom of every page you'll receive, where it will say "Copyright by H. M. Gousha, a division of Simon & Schuster." H. M. Gousha has been publishing *The New Car Cost Guide* since 1956. This is the original pricing guide for new cars, and it has set the standard for timely, accurate, reliable and complete data.

Gousha's *New Car Cost Guide* is used by loan officers in financial institutions, car rental and leasing companies, fleet administrators, insurance adjusters, purchasing agents and other automotive professionals. These people must have accurate pricing data to do their jobs. And both the vehicle manufacturers and their franchised dealers have a vested interest in the ability of these people to do their jobs.

We are a licensee of H. M. Gousha. They keep our pricing data current with regular computer updates.

The Monroney Doctrine

That sticker on the window of every new car is known in car-store jargon as the Monroney, after Oklahoma's Democratic Senator A. S. ("Mike") Monroney, the lawmaker who sponsored the 1958 bill that mandated its presence. (Be sure to refer to it as "the Monroney" early in your negotiations, so the salesman will know he's not dealing with someone who just fell off a turnip truck.)

Monroney's federal law requires that label to include the make, model and identification number of the vehicle; the suggested retail price of the auto and all factory-installed options not included in the base price; and the amount charged to the dealer for delivery to his store.

It's a federal crime to remove or alter that sticker before the vehicle is delivered to the ultimate purchaser. This effectively prevents car stores from replacing the original with a higher-priced sticker if a manufacturer raises the price on subsequent shipments of the same vehicle.

Truck Buyers, Beware

Unfortunately, there's one gaping loophole in the law: It doesn't apply to pickup trucks, which represent about one sixth of the automobile market. In the vast majority of cases, you will find the Monroney label on pickup trucks. But you may run into a few car stores that have replaced the original stickers on some. Manufacturers frequently increase prices during the model year, and some dealers may take advantage of this loophole to change the stickers on their trucks to the latest price, regardless of when they were purchased.

How can you detect this sticker exchange? In a couple of ways. First, look for the EPA label, which contains the federally mandated fuel economy information. This labeling almost always appears on the lower portion of the Monroney sticker, but it may appear legally as a separate label. If a pickup truck's mileage estimates (City MPG and Highway MPG) are on a separate label, there's a chance that the other sticker, with the pricing information, has been changed.

If you have doubts, compare the sticker formats on the new cars on the lot with those on the new trucks. If they differ considerably, that's another indication they may have replaced the Monroneys with their stickers.

How should you deal with suspected sticker switchers? *Our advice would be not to deal with them at all, unless they come clean.* Ask to see the original Monroney. Check the VIN (vehicle identification number) against the one on the car. It's at the base of the front windshield, on top of the dashboard on the driver's side, where the police can find it easily. If they won't cooperate, find a car store with nothing to hide. There will be plenty of them.

In addition to the invoice price, two other factors influence the dealer's real cost. We'll now look at one of them—factory-to-dealer incentives.

THE INCENTIVES GAME

When Chrysler hired Joe Garagiola in the late 1970s to stand up on TV and say, "Buy a car, get a check," he changed the fundamentals of new-car marketing forever. Enticing buyers with direct cash rebates opened a Pandora's box that no one can close.

You'll read periodically that "manufacturers have decided to raise prices by cutting incentives." The number of incentive dollars spent per vehicle tends to rise and fall somewhat with changing market conditions. But as one industry analyst put it, "Incentive programs are like hard drugs; once you get on, it's hard to get off." The consumer has been trained to expect incentives, and fierce competitive pressure will keep them around as long as there's excess production capacity.

U.S. manufacturers spend an estimated $500 to $1,000+ per vehicle on incentives. (In a strong new-vehicle market, the average incentive per car sold will be close to $500; when times are tougher, that number can shoot to more than $1,000.) Even the Japanese, immune from the "incentive disease" for years, now spend similar amounts on incentives, with Nissan and the second- and third-tier companies spending relatively more than Toyota or Honda.

Understand, however, that this $500 to $1,000+ range is an average, spread over all the vehicles sold. Some better-selling cars and trucks almost never need incentives, while other vehicles in a manufacturer's line often carry incentives well above these averages. And some vehicles always seem to have a modest incentive, as a defensive measure against competitors' offers.

Who's paying for this? *You*, the car buyer, of course. *That extra $500 to $1,000+ is simply built into the price of every car sold.* That means you should get the full benefit of that expenditure when you buy a car that carries an incentive.

But wait, there's more to this incentive game than just a check in the mail from Joe Garagiola!

The Other Side of the Incentive Coin

Did you ever sit in front of late-night TV and wonder how so many dealers can shout about "prices below dealer invoice," implying that they're selling them for less than they paid? What they're trying to do, in dealer jargon, is "create a sense of urgency" that will get us off our couches and into their showrooms. The best way to do that, apparently, is to convince us that they're almost giving those things away.

But how can dealers sell cars and trucks for less than they cost? The answer, of course, is that they can't. At least they can't for long and stay in business, and who wants to buy a car from a dealer who's about to go out of business?

So, when they spend all those advertising dollars implying that's what they're doing, are they telling us less than the whole truth or even misleading us? The answer lies somewhere between yes and no. Yes, because a dealer can sell cars all day long for less than he paid for them and still make money. And no, he can't sell cars for less than they cost him without losing money.

What He Paid Is Not What It Costs

Yes, the dealer invoice cost is what he paid for the car. It's the bill he got from the manufacturer, the invoice he had to pay when the auto arrived. But what he paid for the car is not what it ends up costing him because there are several ways manufacturers put money back into his pocket—money that's directly related to the sale of that specific vehicle. One of the ways they do this is through factory-to-dealer incentive programs.

Manufacturers are putting big bucks into these programs. These dollars to dealers can range from $200 up to $2,000 or more per sale on mid-priced vehicles, depending on how badly they want to move the vehicles. (The incentives can get as high as $10,000 on slow-moving luxury cars.)

There's just one problem: Nobody's telling you, the customer, about most of these incentives, yet you're the one who's ultimately paying for them.

The Mushroom Treatment

Since they don't publicize the details of these programs, we're kept in the dark, like mushrooms. All we hear are those commercials telling us to "come on down to take advantage of those [unspecified] factory-to-dealer incentives." There's a good business reason they don't tell us more. And realistically, if you ran a car store, you wouldn't want consumers to know the details, either.

Although this factory money is tied to the sale of a specific vehicle, a dealer may use it for any purpose he wishes. He may pass it along to the customer in the form of a lower price, but that will seldom be his first choice. He'd rather use it to motivate his salesmen, increase his advertising, upgrade his service bays or even paint the building. Most of all, he'd like to pocket it as extra profit, just as you would if you owned a car store.

Here's what the president of one of the world's largest automobile companies had to say on the subject: "A dealer typically says, 'Give me the money, I know how best to use it.' In principle, they always say that. In principle, they're right. But let's face it, [when] we give the money to the customer, it all goes to the customer. Give the money to the dealer, and some of it ends up in the profit of the dealership."

For example, one import manufacturer gave dealers the option of taking incentive money of $1,000 per sale either as dealer cash or as customer rebates. According to the company's national sales manager, only 15 to 20 percent of the dealers opted for the customer rebates. What a surprise!

What you don't know can't hurt the car store. That's the case with factory-to-dealer cash incentives. Why give those factory dollars to people who don't ask for them? And how can we ask if we don't know they exist? According to a *Wall Street Journal* report on one manufacturer's dealer discounts, "As in the past, the money will be paid to dealers instead of consumers, and [the factory] won't publicize the discounts. So buyers will have to bargain for the money, and many might not know the discounts are available."

Believe it or not, some dealers don't tell their own salesmen about these incentives. That's because they want to retain control over how the money is used. That makes good business sense for them, but car buyers are the ones paying the bill. And knowing the details can help them negotiate better.

CarDeals to the Rescue

Fortunately, there is a way for consumers to learn the details of both the customer rebates and the factory-to-dealer incentive programs in effect. It's a four-page report called *CarDeals,* and it's updated every two weeks. (You'll find an abridged version of a typical *CarDeals* report on pages 180–186 of the Appendix.) The information is compiled from "reliable industry sources" by the Center for the Study of Services (CSS), a nonprofit consumer service organization in Washington, DC. Here's what *CarDeals* covers:

Direct-to-Consumer Offers   Although it's relatively easy to learn about factory-to-customer incentive offers, whether they're cash rebates or below-market financing plans, *CarDeals* includes the current details as part of its one-stop incentive information service. In the listing, these customer offers are the ones followed by a "C."

Direct consumer offers are typically either a specific cash rebate amount, or a choice between a cash rebate and a factory-subsidized reduced-rate financing plan, all of which are detailed in the listing. Frequently, you're going to have to decide whether the rebate or the financing plan is better for you. The answer will depend on the size of the rebate, the annual percentage rate (APR) of the factory financing plan, the APRs available from other lenders, the amount you'll be borrowing and the length of the loan.

On pages 187–188 of the Appendix, you'll find a table that will help you compare rebates with financing plans. It was prepared by William Bryan, director of the Bureau of Economic and Business Research at the University of Illinois at Urbana-Champaign. The table lists a range of possible market interest rates down the left side and a range of factory-subsidized rates across the top. It covers loan terms from two to five years. The dollar numbers represent savings per $1,000 of loan amount.

To illustrate how to use this table, let's assume that you were shopping for a Ford Taurus when this issue of *CarDeals* was current. According to the information from *CarDeals* (page 184 of the Appendix), in the Midsize Cars section, a Taurus buyer had the choice of either a $750 to $1,000 cash rebate (depending on the region of the country he or she lived in) or Finance Plan 4, a 7.9 percent APR for up to 48 months (finance plans are detailed on page 186).

Which is more valuable—the rebate or the financing offer? Assume you thought you could buy the Taurus you wanted for about $16,500, including all taxes, title and license fees. You plan to make a 20 percent down payment of $3,300 and borrow the remaining $13,200, paying it off over four years (the maximum term we recommend). Your bank has quoted a 10 percent APR, and the factory plan's rate is 7.9 percent.

The table shows that with a factory-subsidized rate of 8 percent (the closest number to 7.9 percent), you'd save $37.44 per thousand dollars borrowed, or $494.21 over four years (13.2 × $37.44). Since this is less than the $750 rebate, you'd accept the customer cash alternative. As a general rule, rebates of $750 or more usually turn out to be more attractive than the financing alternatives for cars costing under $20,000.

To help us complete our worksheet on the fictitious Speedster wagon on page 69, we've assumed that the All-American Motor Corporation is making the same offer and entered a $750 rebate on the appropriate line.

Important note on sales taxes: Some "how to buy a car" books advise having any rebate credited as a discount in the selling price, as a way to avoid paying sales tax on the amount covered by the rebate. Unfortunately, that advice usually won't work. Most states tax the full sales price before the rebate (and, often, before any trade-in allowance is subtracted). Check your state's tax laws.

Incidentally, some states base the tax on the amended net sales price, after deducting any trade-in allowance. (In theory, you've already paid the tax on the trade-in.) Although this may save you a few hundred dollars in taxes on the new vehicle, you're still likely to come out ahead by selling your current car yourself at retail, instead of trading it in at wholesale.

Before leaving this section, we should add that there are some direct-to-consumer offers that don't appear on the *CarDeals* report. These fall into two categories. The first are special additional rebates, typically $500 or so, that automakers offer to first-time car buyers or recent college graduates. These offers are usually from Ford, GM or Chrysler, though you may occasionally find similar rebate offers from import makes because they make good business sense. If a company can sell you an entry-level vehicle, it probably has a better chance of attracting you to its higher-priced models in later years. If you're in either of these categories, you should ask about these programs. The money comes from the manufacturer's pocket, not the dealer's.

Another kind of offer worth asking about is a discount for people who own a car of the same make, or people who have *ever* owned a car of the same make. Some of the smaller import brands make these offers, since a good percentage of their sales comes from previous customers. As one Fighting Chance customer reported to us, "When I called Saab's 800 number to ask for information, they sent me a coupon good for $750 if I purchased a new Saab by the end of the month." These offers don't happen often, but if you're shopping for a make you've owned before, it's always a good idea to make the phone call and ask the question.

Direct-to-Dealer Offers   Now let's look at the money manufacturers pay dealers to sell cars to you. These harder-to-uncover dealer incentives are followed by a "D" in the *CarDeals* listing. As you review these programs, the Center for the Study of Services suggests that you keep the following points in mind:

• *Some of these programs pay dealers more money per car as they sell more cars during the program period.* Unless otherwise noted, when you see a range in the listing (for example, the $800–$1,600 range shown for Isuzu pickup trucks on page 185 of the Appendix), this means that a dealer gets more cash per car if he sells more cars.

- *In some programs, all dealers have the same volume targets.* That means you can expect larger dealers to get bigger cash payments than smaller dealers, simply because they'll sell more cars. Everything else being equal, you should be able to negotiate a better deal with a large dealer during these programs.

- *In other programs, large dealers must meet higher volume targets than small dealers to qualify for incentive cash,* so there's no reason to expect a better deal at a large dealership.

- To help you differentiate these program types, the *CarDeals* listing tells you which ones are based on sales targets set for each dealer, as opposed to targets that are the same for all dealers. As an example, see the generous Nissan Maxima program shown in the Midsize Cars section on page 184 of the Appendix. Dealers received from $1,000 to $1,500 per car, based on individual sales targets. If a dealer met those targets by September 2, the end of the promotion period, he would get cash for all Maximas sold in the period.

- Returning to our pricing worksheet on the fictitious Speedster wagon on page 69, let's assume that All-American Motor Corporation's dealers can earn factory cash up to an extra $200 per vehicle, based on individual sales targets. You'll note that we've added that $200 to the Factory-to-Dealer Incentives line on the chart.

We'll discuss in Chapter 20 exactly how to use this dealer incentive information to your advantage during the negotiating process, along with the previously outlined dealer invoice cost data. For now, let's just say that since you're the one who ultimately *pays* for it, you're entitled to the benefit, and there's bound to be a dealer or two who'll want to sell you a car badly enough to agree.

Living Proof: Vehicle Options Can Be Valuable

With a current issue of *CarDeals* you can examine the listing to see whether any of your finalist vehicles are covered by incentive programs. That's when you may discover a very tangible benefit of keeping more than one car on your list. It's not unusual at any time for the maker of one car to be offering a consumer and/or dealer incentive of $500 to $1,000 or more, while the maker of a similar car offers less, or none at all. That difference may be just what it takes to make one car the best choice for you.

To illustrate, let's assume you were interested in buying a Toyota Corolla sedan. Turn to page 183 of the Appendix. You'll see in the Subcompacts section that there was a factory-to-dealer cash offer on the Corolla ranging from $800 to $1,000, based on sales targets set for each dealer. But the virtually identical Geo Prizm, made in the same plant in Fremont, California, offered a direct customer rebate of $1,500. In addition, the Prizm carried a sticker price several hundred dollars below the comparable Corolla. Knowing that, you might find the Geo to be a very appealing alternative.

If you've got your heart set on just one vehicle, and it isn't covered by a current program, you should consider waiting a month or two. New programs start all the time. Remember, though, that many better-selling cars and trucks almost never have incentives.

As you look over the sample *CarDeals* report, remember that you may obtain the current issue directly from us. It will be part of the information package that contains the up-to-date dealer invoice prices and the current sales and inventory picture for the vehicles you're considering. See Chapter 24 for ordering instructions.

Now let's turn to the third factor that determines the real dealer cost.

DEALER HOLDBACK (THE MONEY NO ONE TALKS ABOUT)

The final piece of this cost puzzle is called "dealer holdback," and no one talks about it. If the invoice cost is the last thing the salesman wants you to know, holdback is the last thing the dealer wants you to know, right behind factory-to-dealer incentives. Chances are, he doesn't even discuss it with his salesmen because it's the last thing he wants them thinking about. For most makes, both domestics and imports, holdback is one of the most significant ways manufacturers put money back into dealers' pockets.

What Is This Thing No One Discusses Openly?

Holdback is a specific percentage of a vehicle's price that is built into the original factory invoice price the dealer pays, held back by the manufacturer for a while, then credited back to the dealer's account after the vehicles are sold, typically quarterly. General Motors, Ford and Chrysler each hold back an amount equal to 3 percent of the retail sticker price (MSRP). While this percentage may seem relatively small, the dollars involved can be significant because even a mid-priced new vehicle costs so much today.

For example, a Dodge dealer could take a sedan with a $15,000 sticker, sell it at his invoice price and still make $450 from holdback. A Ford dealer could part with a $30,000 sport/utility vehicle at dealer invoice and still realize $900 in holdback on the deal. And a Cadillac dealer could unload a $40,000 luxury car at invoice and receive a holdback credit from GM of $1,200.

In effect, holdback is a discount to the dealer which reduces the cost of the vehicle below an inflated dealer invoice price. Think of it as boomerang bucks, money he sends the factory when he pays the original invoice, but which eventually comes back to him.

Because he pays it out up front, he treats it as if it were a cost item, instead of the profit item it really represents when he gets it back from the factory. Since it's a hidden item, it's excluded from the sales transaction. That means he doesn't have to pay a sales commission on it, and it's not on the table for a buyer to negotiate away.

Holdback was instituted in the early 1960s, we understand, as a way to ensure that dealers would have money on hand to pay Uncle Sam at tax time. While that may be one of several benefits to a dealer, holdback clearly benefits manufacturers as well. They've got the use of that money, interest-free, until the next quarterly payment. (In return, they give the dealer an extra couple of weeks to pay for cars received.) And if a dealer owes them money he won't or can't pay, they've always got a chunk of his on hand to cover some of that debt.

Few dealers ever share any of this holdback profit with customers. They count on it to pay overhead expenses. But telling them you know about it helps you keep them in their cage, making it more difficult for them to claim they aren't making money on your transaction. In effect, it gives you firmer ground to stand on.

It's Not Just a Detroit Accounting Item

The practice of holdback has spread to most import brands. Based on the best inside information available, here are the holdback policies by manufacturer:

• Some automakers hold back a percentage of the full sticker price (MSRP). Like all Ford, General Motors and Chrysler divisions, Saab, Subaru and Rolls Royce hold back 3 percent of the sticker price. For BMW, Jaguar, Nissan and Volkswagen, holdback is 2 percent of the MSRP.

- Others hold back a percentage of the base sticker price (MSRP), excluding the destination charge and the price of any additional option packages and accessories. For Acura, Honda, Mazda, Infiniti and Lexus, holdback is 2 percent of the base sticker price.

- A few manufacturers hold back a percentage of the base dealer invoice price, excluding the destination charge and the price of any additional option packages and accessories. Mercedes-Benz, Porsche and Toyota hold back 2 percent of the base dealer invoice. Hyundai's holdback is either 2 percent of the base sticker or 2 percent of the base dealer invoice price.

- Volvo's holdback is a standard $800 per vehicle.

- For all of the makes mentioned above, the holdback is built into the dealer invoice price. There are two makes that don't build it in, but add it to the invoice price at the point of purchase. Isuzu adds 3 percent of the base sticker price (MSRP), and Mitsubishi adds 2 percent of the base sticker price.

- We believe that all automakers have holdback, but we can't confirm it for any makes not mentioned above.

We'll discuss in Chapter 20 exactly how to use your knowledge of holdback during the negotiating process. Now, though, return to the sample worksheet for our All-American Speedster on page 69. We've assumed that the fictitious All-American Motor Corporation has the same holdback policy as the three actual domestic manufacturers, and we've entered $532 on the holdback line (3 percent of the $17,720 suggested retail price, excluding the destination charge).

The dealer invoice price. Factory incentives. Holdback. Those are the three key elements that determine the real cost of the vehicle.

There's one other major factor that comes into play each year, after the new models have been introduced. It's called a year-end carryover allowance, another kind of factory-to-dealer payment that we'll discuss in the next chapter.

Many that are first shall be last;
and the last shall be first.
                    —Matthew 19:30

Timing

Is Money

Success in any serious endeavor can have a lot to do with being in the right place at the right time. For the new car buyer, timing is money. There are so many timing-related issues in the auto shopping process that we've prepared a separate chapter to focus your attention on all of them.

In this race, getting there last often beats getting there first. Here are some specific illustrations of how the tortoise beats the hare:

1. DON'T MILK THAT DEALER-INCENTIVE COW TILL JUST BEFORE MIDNIGHT

If one of your finalists is covered by a current factory-to-dealer cash incentive program, you'll turn to the *CarDeals* report and check the program's end date. Then you'll time all your serious price negotiation visits so that you'll be able to sign the sales agreement *on one of the last two or three eligible days.*

Here's why: Every promotion program has a beginning, middle and end. As the end approaches, there's a lot of pressure to pump out every sale possible. That's because these programs are often structured so that dealers get higher incentive payments as the number of cars sold increases.

You want to buy from a dealer who's at the highest cash incentive plateau. Your purchase might even be the one that pushes a dealer's entire sales organization up to that plateau. In some programs, a dealer that reaches a certain sales target gets extra cash for all cars sold in the promotion period. This could mean hundreds of dollars for each car previously sold! That store might give quite dramatic discounts as it gets close to its target. That store might be ripe for a knowledgeable shopper to negotiate the buy of a lifetime!

As we noted in the previous chapter, if one or more of your finalist vehicles isn't covered by a consumer or dealer incentive program today, consider waiting a month or two, if you can. New programs start all the time, and you might save an extra thousand dollars or more if you can make one of them work for you.

2. THE END OF THE LINE CAN BE A GREAT PLACE TO STAND

Many people like to buy at the end of the model year, during those year-end cleanout sales. The new models are about to arrive, and they've got to make space for them.

One reason prices are friendlier then is that some manufacturers provide extra money to their dealers to help them sell those year-end leftovers. (They won't get heavy orders for new models if dealers are loaded with last year's cars.) This extra money is called a "carryover allowance," and it's a practice employed most often by Detroit.

General Motors and Ford regularly provide a carryover allowance of 5 percent of the sticker price (that's 5 percent of MSRP, not 5 percent of dealer invoice), which they credit to dealers for every previous year's vehicle sold after the new model of the same vehicle arrives in the showroom. On a car or truck with a $20,000 sticker price, that 5 percent represents an additional $1,000 for you to bargain for.

Chrysler has traditionally shunned carryover allowances. Several years ago, it offered its dealers the choice of a 5 percent carryover allowance *or* participation in the July–September consumer and dealer incentive programs. As you might expect, the carryover allowance had few takers among dealers, whose basic credo is, "Sell it now and worry about tomorrow later."

Import makes don't use across-the-line carryover allowances, but many of them place hefty factory-to-dealer cash incentives on last year's models of selected vehicles.

One Key Closeout Issue: Slim Pickings

Sometimes year-end pickings can be quite slim, even in a down market. If sales have been depressed for months, both manufacturers and their dealers may write off a model year when it's only half over. Dealers get very selective with their orders as the current year's production winds down, and the factories structure their buildout plans to allow dealers to maintain lean inventories of only the fastest-moving models. They're both hoping to end the old-model year without a glut of leftovers, so they can focus all their resources on the new-model launch in the fall.

This occasional attack of sanity among car makers is not necessarily good news for shoppers looking for end-of-year bargains. But more often than not, if your heart's set on a model-year leftover, you'll have many to choose from—assuming there are two or three finalists you'd be happy to drive home. Look through the sample *CarDeals* report, printed on pages 180–186 of the Appendix. You'll note many incentive offers for last year's models of Ford and Mercury vehicles, along with the accompanying carryover allowance notation: "and 5% of list price (D)." Those offers wouldn't be there if all last year's models had been sold.

The Other Side of the Year-End Coin

Don't be blinded by those apparently great year-end clearance deals. Savvy buyers understand that they are a mixed blessing. There's a reason Detroit pays its dealers a carryover allowance for last year's cars in inventory after the new models arrive: They're worth considerably less then. Indeed, it's proper to question whether 5 percent of the sticker price is a large enough allowance to cover a vehicle's precipitous drop in value after the new models are introduced.

The day the new models arrived, that old model became last year's car. A year later, when next year's models come out, it'll be a two-year-old. If you sell it then, it will have taken a two-year depreciation hit in one year, no matter how much TLC you've lavished on it.

You should be especially cautious buying last year's closeout if there have been extensive styling changes in the new model. That old, out-of-style car will depreciate even faster than normal when there's a much prettier successor on the highway.

The only way anyone should buy last year's model after the new models arrive is at a big discount from dealer invoice. You should get the entire carryover allowance (5 percent of MSRP) plus all the customer and dealer incentive dollars. Even then, you should plan to keep that car for several years to ride out the negative effect of the car's lower real value when it was purchased.

The moral of the story is that year-end is a great time to buy a bargain, as long as you don't have to sell it in a year or two. And when you trade it, you should do it for another year-end closeout model so you don't get stuck selling low and buying high.

Returning to the worksheet for our imaginary All-American Speedster on page 69, you'll note that we entered an assumed year-end carryover allowance of $911 on the appropriate line. (That's 5 percent of the $18,220 sticker price.) If you were shopping for that car after the new model arrived, that 5 percent would be an important element in your negotiation.

3. GETTING THERE FIRST CAN BE AN EXPENSIVE TRIP

Remember the Mazda MX-5 Miata. (That's a warning, not a question.) The Miata was introduced with rave reviews, with a sticker price of $13,800 and just enough cars to reach from your kitchen to your dining room, end to end. Mazda dealers loved it! Many put their ADM (additional dealer markup) stickers on every one and doubled or tripled their gross profit per car. And the newspapers were still full of consumers' buy-and-sell offers at prices from $20,000. Talk about being in new-car heat!

Today you can buy a Miata for a few hundred dollars over the dealer invoice price, and have just as much fun driving it as the folks who paid an extra $5,000 or $10,000 when it was introduced. You just can't be the first on your block to own one.

Supply and Demand: It's the Law

Whatever the item, if more people want it than can get it, those who get it will pay for the privilege. World Series tickets, Super Bowl hotel rooms, the first 2,000 Mazda Miatas . . . you name it.

This truth works against the car buyer at the beginning of the model year, though usually less dramatically than in the case of a hot new car like the Miata. From October through December, when a new model is in relatively short supply, the dealer may not accept the same price he will later in the year, when the only things standing in line are the cars on his lot.

Bugs Aren't Just on Windshields

There's another reason to avoid a brand-new model in the early months of production: bugs. Even in this era of dramatically improved product quality, it frequently takes auto manufacturers several months or more to get the hang of making glitch-free products.

Look at the vexing little problems that plagued GM's Saturn in its first year: A recall for defective seats. A recall for a corrosive engine coolant. Early buyers' complaints about noisy, vibrating engines.

Saturn was launched with great ballyhoo, following a $5 billion capital investment and seven years of meticulous planning. Yet many say that what Saturn did best in its first year was correct problems with great consumer and public relations sensitivity.

By Saturn's second year, the bugs had been eliminated and the Saturn buyer could anticipate a glitch-free vehicle. But Saturn's early pratfalls illustrate that even a company determined to get it right can stumble coming out of the blocks. And the wise buyer will always count to ten before purchasing a brand-new vehicle.

4. TALK TURKEY LATE IN THE MONTH, AND LATE IN THE DAY

As it says in the song, "There is a time to every purpose under heaven."

- The time to kick tires and take test drives and do research is during the first three weeks of the month.
- The time for serious negotiation is during the last week of the month.

Every sales organization lives or dies from month to month. Auto manufacturers report sales monthly, and they focus their dealers on the same time frame, using quotas or incentives or just plain fear to motivate them. The dealers pass along the quotas, the incentives and the fear to their sales managers.

That usually makes the end of the month the best time to buy. Your purchase could be the one that puts them over the top, and you might strike a terrific bargain.

Some of the smartest shoppers always buy their new cars during the last hour of the last day of December. That way salesmen can't waste their time with their system games. (More on these in the next chapter.) They carry a cashier's check for the maximum amount they're prepared to pay. And they claim they always leave with both the car they want and the dealer's check for the difference between their maximum and the lower price they really paid.

Here's another tactic that works. If it's the last weekend of the month, and your price negotiation is stalled on a number that's too high, tell the salesman that you're going home to sleep on it, that you'll be back next weekend. Many times you'll find that the price will drop magically, just as you head for the door.

The exception to this end-of-month rule would be if the last days of a relevant factory-to-dealer incentive program came at a different time. Given all the incentive activity in the market today, there's probably more buyer leverage in timing those specific factory programs just right. (You'll note, however, that most programs seem to finish at the end of a month, or a few days later.)

5. AN EMPTY SHOWROOM CAN BE FULL OF OPPORTUNITY

If you're the only one there, your chances of striking a terrific deal may be enhanced dramatically. So don't be afraid to shop "the middles"—the middle of the week, the middle of a blizzard or deluge, even the middle of the Christmas season (as long as you don't tell them it's a Christmas present). And car stores can be particularly accommodating in January and February, when most people are paying off holiday bills and not thinking of buying new cars and trucks.

6. AT TENT SALES, YOU GET GREAT DEALS ON CAMELS, NOT CARS

The timing elements to ignore are the corny sales events dealers love to advertise. In car-salesman lingo, their purpose is always to create a sense of urgency, to get prospects into showrooms by implying that this gigantic tent sale is the opportunity of a lifetime . . . and when it's over, it's over. Sure it is. Until next month's red tag sale, or the following month's midnight madness sale or Presidents' Day sale or overstock clearance sale.

The transaction prices at most of these phony events are no lower than they were before the sale. They are probably higher, because those ads attract gullible people who believe that a car dealer's advertised sale is as real as a department store's advertised sale. Unless the ads feature some specific offer, such as a manufacturer's below-market financing program, the only real opportunities there are for salesmen to take advantage of folks who fall for the come-on. So if there's a midsummer heat wave in your town and the beat-the-heat sale ads promise free air conditioning with every car sold, you should extend your antennae fully. For a mid-priced vehicle, that air conditioner costs the dealer more than his profit on a typical sale to a knowledgeable buyer. Unless it's supplied free by the manufacturer, assume that you're paying for any "free" equipment. If the dealer giveth, the dealer also taketh away.

7. "THE STRONGEST OF WARRIORS ARE THESE TWO: TIME AND PATIENCE." (Leo Tolstoy, *War and Peace*)

If you forget everything else in this chapter, remember this: Time is always on your side, not theirs. In a waiting game, the loser will be the one who needs the deal the most. The sooner you need to have a new car, the more it's going to cost. If that's today, or this weekend, you'd better have a Brink's truck for a trade-in. A loaded Brink's truck. But if you can wait 'em out, the time will come when they'll want a sale even more than you want a new car. That offer they refused weeks ago has a way of looking much better in the cold, hard glare of the end of another month. Sometimes just one more sale—even a below-invoice sale—can be very important to a dealer.

All it takes is time, a luxury that dealers seldom have. If you've got it, use it.

16

We must take a hard look at the way we market our cars . . . and the way we approach customers on the floor and present the deal. Until we address these issues, the image of new-car dealers will remain about the same—awful.
—President of the National Automobile Dealers Association, at a convention in Dallas

The Games Salesmen Play

Before you finalize your approach to negotiating price, you should be aware of some of the things car salesmen do to control the sales situation and to get you to do what they want, which is to buy today, at a price that maximizes their profit. Watch for these old favorites:

THE BUDDY SYSTEM

This salesman is on your side; it's you and him against "them." He'll do his best to get management to give you a great deal. He leaves the room a lot, only to return to say they wouldn't buy a price that low, they need more. (You're at the blood bank, negotiating with Dracula through a zombie, and the only blood there is yours.)

This is a game, and a transparent one at that. Don't let him play it. Tell him you appreciate his concern for you, but you want to talk to "them," not their messenger. If the game doesn't stop, walk out.

THE SILENT TREATMENT

This is the Buddy System's first cousin. The salesman leaves you in the room (they call it "the box") for long periods of time while he's "negotiating for you" with his sales manager.

In reality, that salesman probably knows exactly how low they'll go to sell you that car. While he's away you can bet he's drinking coffee with the guys, talking about last night's date or next week's fishing trip. He'll eventually come back with a "bump" (an increase) over your last offer, because "they" didn't buy it.

The game here is to keep you there (so you can't be at any other car store) and to wear you down. They want you so frustrated by the delays that you'll sign anything just to get it finished.

The first time he gets up to leave, tell him nicely but firmly that you've been through this before, that you appreciate the position he's in, but you're not going to sit there for a lot of back-and-forth negotiations with a phantom. Say that if he's not back in five minutes with someone you can negotiate with directly, you've got three other dealers you plan to visit and he can expect to find you gone. Then look him straight in the eye and hit the beeper on your digital wristwatch.

THE BUMP-AND-GRIND

This is a more systematic version of the Silent Treatment. The waiting periods aren't as long, but you're being played up and down like a yo-yo by someone you don't even get to see.

Your buddy, the salesman, leaves the box after introducing you to his sales manager, who'll be "the closer." (You've been T.O.'d, or taken over, by a more senior salesman.) This guy is usually still a middleman, taking your concessions out to some phantom who scribbles notes you can't read and returning to ask if you can "just help him out" to the tune of another $50 a month so he can close the deal. (Over four years, that $50 a month will cost you $2,400, and the closer will get 10 to 25 percent of that "bump.")

Your response to the Bump-and-Grind should be the same as to the Silent Treatment. Either it stops now or you walk to another car store, now.

THE LOWBALL OPENER

Some stores will have the salesman quote you an initial price that sounds too good to be true—sometimes over the phone, as a way to get you into the showroom. *You can be sure that it is.* When you agree to that number, he'll return with a "bump," saying they wouldn't go for it. This is just another way to draw you into the game.

If you think he's lowballing, tell him that you've been through this before, that you expect him to return again and say management wouldn't buy it, and that if that's the game they want to play, you've got three other stores to visit and you'll leave as soon as he returns with the predicted news flash.

Tell him that you want to talk to someone who can negotiate with you directly, now, or you're leaving.

Note: Another variation is the Lowball Send-off. The salesman knows you're going to go out and shop around, so he gives you an unrealistically low quote that no dealer would match, including his. When you leave, he's got you "out on a ball," and he knows you'll be back. When you eventually return to take him up on that lowball offer, you learn that it was too good to be true. By then, he hopes, you'll be so tired of running around trying to beat it that you'll be ready to make any deal he wants.

THE CASTING DIRECTOR

This salesman wants to typecast you as soon as he can. Anything you say will be used against you.

• Are you "a payment buyer," someone who cares only that the monthly payment is something you can handle? He can fix you right up, with a deal that maximizes both his profit and the length of your loan. (But the monthly payments will be close to what you said you could handle.)

Don't ever talk to a car salesman about monthly payments. If you've done your homework, you already know what kind of financing and payments you're planning, and it's none of his business.

- Are you "an allowance buyer," someone who's focused only on the trade-in allowance they'll offer on your used car? He can fix you right up, with a deal that maximizes both your trade-in allowance and his profit.

Don't ever talk to a car salesman about a trade-in allowance. Go back and review Chapters 4 through 9. By now, you're too smart to fall for this one. As you've already learned, the less you tell the salesman, the better off you'll be.

THE CHECK-IN CLERK

In many dealerships, the first thing a salesman will want to do is fill out a data card, with your name, address and phone numbers. He'll add the sticker price information on the car you want, including all the options. Then he'll want to add information about your trade-in, like the vehicle identification number and the mileage.

Then, as long as he's writing, he'll ask your date of birth, driver's license number and social security number. (They'll need this to run a credit report on you if you end up financing through the dealer. But they want to run the report now, both to be sure you're not a deadbeat and to see which other dealers have checked your credit recently, so they'll know where you've been shopping.)

No deal has been discussed yet, no prices mentioned, but he wants all this personal information. He'll pass the data card to his superior as soon as he leaves the box.

This is a car store, not a hotel or personnel office! And you're not registering for a room or applying for a job. At this stage, you're just starting a dialogue that might or might not lead to a purchase. *Until you've got a deal that you can agree to, all you should tell him is your name.* Even if you end up buying there, they won't need most of that information unless you're financing through the dealer.

THE HOSTAGE TAKER

Many salesmen will ask for a deposit check to accompany your offer when they take it to their superior. They call it evidence that you're a serious buyer. But for them, *that check is a hostage that will keep you at their store and prevent you from shopping around for a better deal.*

Smile nicely, but tell him that you're not writing a deposit check for anything until you and they have agreed on a deal for everything. And that if his store requires a deposit check simply to negotiate a deal, you're sure you can find one that doesn't. The rule will change quickly.

Incidentally, the keys to your current car can also become an effective hostage. Salesmen have been known to "misplace" them, and even to refuse to return them when you ask. At this point you're not there to talk about a trade-in; *keep the keys in your pocket or purse.*

THE LIMITED-TIME OFFER

You might negotiate to a price that sounds pretty good, but this is only your first store. You plan to go through the same drill at two or three other dealerships. You tell him that it's a big decision for you, that you want to think about it overnight. You thank him and get up to leave. The salesman then says, in a bit of a huff, that if you leave he can't give you the same price tomorrow. (He's upset; his mission is to close you now.)

Call his bluff! Smile and say that's too bad, because if it's true he's going to miss the opportunity to sell you a car. You are leaving, you've got several other dealers you haven't talked with yet, and you're sure one of them will have a different attitude.

Then ask him again if he really meant that he wouldn't sell you that car at that price tomorrow, so you'll be sure not to bother him.

Remember Reality 101: There's another deal that good, and probably better, around the next corner.

Then remember Salesman's Reality 101: If you don't buy, he doesn't sell. And if he doesn't sell, he doesn't eat.

MR. OBNOXIOUS

Chances are, you'll end up with a given salesman just because it's his turn. His number is up when you walk in, and you become his "up."

Chemistry is important. If you quickly find he's someone you'd rather not deal with, excuse yourself to go to the rest room. Then ask someone where you can find the sales manager, walk in and tell him you've got a problem he's going to have to solve, or you're going to have to leave. That salesman is not someone you can work with, and you'd like to talk to someone else. Then go to the rest room.

When you return, you'll meet a new, less obnoxious salesperson—maybe even the sales manager himself.

If a Cavalier is advertised for $7,999, you had better load it up with extras or your head is on the chopping block.

—Salesperson participating in a sales certification training program developed by the National Automobile Dealers Association (quoted in *Automotive News*)

Back-End Options: Just Say No

The *Random House Webster's College Dictionary* defines "option" as "the power or right of choosing." "Optional" is also defined as meaning "not required."

Car salesmen have a different dictionary. Theirs defines "option" as "any additional equipment or accessories they can stick on a new vehicle that are of maximum profitability to the car store."

It's bad enough that manufacturers load their vehicles with packages of optional equipment, some of which you may not need or want. At least they typically give you a package price, so that you're not paying that much for the things you don't want.

But then the car stores add their own high-profit dealer options on the back end. You'll find them hung all over the vehicles you're shopping. That doesn't mean you have to buy them.

THE OTHER STICKER

Your first clue that something's up is the other sticker on the window. It's often designed to look just like the Monroney, complete with an illustration of that little gas pump. It's not; *it's the car store's sticker.*

There's often more profit potential for the car store on that sticker than on the basic car itself, but most of the items there won't add a dime's worth of value or utility. Let's replay a few of the Greatest Hits.

"The Mop 'n Glow"

This group includes things like "rust-preventive undercoating," "fabric guard protection spray," "paint sealant," "sound shield," decorative striping, mud flaps and deluxe floor mats. This strange entourage frequently masquerades under important-sounding names like Optional Environmental Protection Package.

This little protection package can carry a retail price from $300–$400 to as much as $1,000 or more. Its cost to the car store is peanuts—typically under $100. You need this stuff like a moose needs a hat rack!

• Let's start with *"rust-preventive undercoating."* Today's new vehicles carry very substantial anti-corrosion warranties from just about all manufacturers. The domestics typically cover 6 or 7 years, or 100,000 miles, whichever comes first. The major imports cover 5 to 7 years, usually with unlimited mileage. (Check the coverage for your finalists.)

Probably the best argument against buying dealer rustproofing is that many factories recommend against it! Here's a quote from a General Motors warranty:

> Some after-manufacture rustproofing may create a potential environment which reduces the corrosion resistance designed and built into your vehicle. Depending upon application technique, [it] could result in damage or failure of some electrical or mechanical systems of your vehicle. Repairs to correct damage or mal-

functions caused by after-manufacture rustproofing are not covered under any of your GM new vehicle warranties.

Any questions?

- *"Fabric guard protection spray."* You call this Scotchgard. A 14-ounce can of 3M's Scotchgard® sells for a few dollars in your supermarket and covers 14 to 21 square feet of fabric. Three cans should do the trick.

- *"Paint sealant."* Today's automotive paint jobs are technological wonders compared to twenty years ago, when additional protection may have been beneficial. The primary thing it benefits now is the size of the salesmen's bonus pool.

The bottom line: Tell the salesman to leave the Mop 'n Glow in Aisle 9, where it belongs. Tell him either he throws in the $79.95 cost of the total package for free or finds you a car without it, or you'll find another dealer who will. (In fact, you'd rather buy a car without it.)

Dealer Preparation

You may see a charge for dealer preparation. You shouldn't pay it. Virtually all manufacturers include predelivery preparation in the car's base price.

ADM, ADP and AMV

Printed boldly on the Other Sticker, these abbreviations represent the most arrogant form of customer-fleecing. They stand for additional dealer markup, additional dealer profit and additional market value. They used to be added to any car in relatively high demand and short supply, particularly imports.

In today's tough sales climate, most car stores have dropped these extra charges, but they're not extinct. You'll find them on virtually all new vehicles at some stores. The added markups can range from $1,000 on a compact pickup truck to $5,000 or more on an expensive sports car. What they provide, of course, is an artificially higher asking price from which to start negotiating.

If you see them, tell the salesman you're going to ignore them. If he won't cooperate, either you've got a dealer who's not living in the real world or you're looking at the rare vehicle whose demand exceeds today's supply (like that Dodge Viper which the dealer thought would sell for $20,000 over the sticker price).

Our advice would be to shop several dealers to find one without "A-words" on his stickers, or to wait a few months for supply to catch up with demand. (It always does.) And remember that a car sold with an "A-word" sticker won't be worth a nickel more at trade-in time than the same car without that initial surcharge.

Some Options are Hard to Avoid

Some options, both manufacturer- and dealer-installed, just seem to come with the territory. That's often true on newer models that are in relatively short supply. For example, for a while it was difficult to find a Honda Accord station wagon without a relatively expensive dealer-installed roof rack. If you were a prospect for that car, you learned to grin and bear it. What's a station wagon without a roof rack, anyway?

Here's one option you should avoid: the car store's logo, either drilled into or glued onto the back end of your new car. Make sure you tell the salesman you won't accept delivery of any vehicle with his store's advertising attached to it. (The exception to this rule is a license frame plate bearing the dealer's name, which you can remove easily. As you'll learn in Chapter 19, this can be a useful long-term ally.)

INDIVIDUAL FACTORY ORDERS: THE SOLUTION TO THE OPTION GAME?

As you may know, domestic cars can be special-ordered from the manufacturers. Many advisors recommend this as the way to get a vehicle equipped exactly to your order. And perhaps there is something special about having one built just for you.

Any dealer would be happy to take your order. It's an easy sale and, unlike his regular inventory, he doesn't have to invest anything in your car. He may even accept a low-profit deal, just because it'll help his "turn and earn" record. (Many dealers are allotted cars based on past sales performance. Moving a lot of cars, especially in a poor sales year, will help ensure that he'll get all he needs in better years, when popular cars are scarcer and markups are higher.)

Nevertheless, we don't think special ordering is the best way to buy a car under most circumstances, for these reasons:

✔ For openers, it'll take 6 to 8 weeks or more to get delivery, if you're lucky. A lot of things can happen to your current car in that time, none of them good.

✔ You may not be able to predict a realistic delivery date, especially if you order in the second half of the model year. When sales are slower, manufacturers periodically shut down selected factories for a week or more to avoid excess inventory buildup. The plants selected may include the one that makes your car.

✔ It's not as easy as it used to be to get the exact options you want, even with a factory order. Manufacturers don't really customize orders. Many of them sell certain popular options only in packages, which may contain things you don't want.

✔ You probably won't be able to take advantage of either consumer or dealer incentive offers with a factory-ordered car. The consumer programs typically require that you take delivery from dealer stock, and the dealer programs are usually for cars sold and delivered within certain dates. So you'll pay the $500 to $1,000+ built into the price of the car to cover these programs, but you'll receive no benefit.

✔ If you're adamant about getting a specifically equipped car, and if the car is built that way, a dealer may be able to find that exact car for you at another dealership. All dealers have access to a computerized inventory of vehicles in their sales zone, which generally covers several states. They frequently work a dealer exchange to get a specific car. (Note, however, that on a dealer trade, the dealer who sends the car retains the factory holdback dollars on the vehicle. That may mean that your dealer—the receiving dealer—will be less flexible on price than he would be for a vehicle from his own inventory.)

✔ Finally, we think you've got a better shot at negotiating an attractive price on a car that's in a dealer's stock than on a special-ordered car. He's paying interest to keep that car in inventory, so he's highly motivated to get it off his lot and into your garage.

Here's how to estimate how long a car has been in a dealer's inventory. Look for the federally mandated manufacturer's sticker or plate that shows the month and year of manufacture. It will also carry these words: "This vehicle conforms to all applicable federal motor vehicle safety, bumper and theft prevention standards in effect on the date of manufacture shown above." It's usually placed inside the jamb of the driver's door, but may also be under the hood—on the firewall between the engine and passenger compartments—or on one of the wheel wells.

If the date of manufacture was more than four months ago, you may assume the dealer is particularly anxious to sell that vehicle and might accept a lower offer than for a car that just arrived on his lot.

SOMETIMES A FACTORY ORDER IS A TERRIFIC IDEA

We have learned from customers of our Fighting Chance information service that a factory order often can save you a lot of money if you're shopping for a hot-selling vehicle that's in short supply.

New cars are nothing but high-priced commodities, and pricing flexibility is determined by supply and demand. Because there are many more makers and models and dealers than we really need, supply always exceeds demand for most vehicles. But almost always, there are a few "hot" models where supply trails demand.

Ours is a fad-driven culture, in part, and public interest in a given product can increase dramatically overnight. If that product is a lipstick color or a clothing style, manufacturers can turn on a dime to meet the demand. But the lead time required to react to changes in demand for automobiles is seldom measured in weeks or months. And whenever a dealer gets fewer units of a vehicle than he can sell, he will demand—and get—higher prices.

There are two ways to beat a sticky price situation. One is to postpone your purchase for a few months. Supply always exceeds demand eventually. The alternative is to order one from the factory. Many customers report buying vehicles in short supply for a few hundred dollars over the dealer's invoice by placing a special order. The dealer puts up no money (he'll get a deposit from you, typically about $1,000), and it's a quick, no-brainer sale, so he's often willing to settle for a slim profit, plus holdback, of course. Most important, he doesn't have to burn his slim inventory on someone who's done some homework; he can save it for the idiot who will walk in after you and pay him the sticker price or more to buy a scarce vehicle. The down side, of course, is that you'll wait 2 or 3 months for your new toy to arrive.

18

Are Extended Warranties Warranted?

The sale of an extended warranty contract, which pays for repairs that occur after the factory warranty runs out, is a big back-end profit item for every car store. These contracts typically cost $500 to $1,000 and can exceed $2,000, depending on what they cover and what the traffic (you) will bear.

You can expect to get a strong recommendation to buy one, frequently from the store's F&I manager. Watch out for this guy. You've escaped from the "closing box," but you're in the clutches of another commissioned salesman. He's a low-pressure operator who wants you to trust his advice as you would your father's. He's not your father; he's interested in your wallet, not your welfare.

BE PREPARED FOR THIS ONE

You should determine beforehand whether this purchase makes sense for you. The decision hinges on your answers to these two questions:

1. What's the basic bumper-to-bumper warranty on the car you're buying?

2. How long do you plan to keep the car, and about how many miles will you drive it?

MOST BASIC WARRANTIES ARE NOW CLOSE TO PARITY

The old standard, a bumper-to-bumper warranty of one year or 12,000 miles (whichever comes first), is a thing of the past, thanks to Toyota, Honda and Nissan. The Japanese Big Three provide a basic warranty of 3 years or 36,000 miles, and starting with the 1992 models, Detroit's Big Three finally matched their key competitors. (Ford and Chrysler maintained that ancient 12-month/12,000-mile warranty on most vehicles through the 1991 model year.)

The basic bumper-to-bumper warranty covers most parts of the car. An additional powertrain warranty covers the things that make the car go (the engine, transmission and drivetrain), frequently for a longer period than the basic warranty. And a longer corrosion warranty covers actual holes in the body caused by rust. (Separate warranties cover the battery, tires and other accessory items you may add to the vehicle.)

The warranties in effect as we're writing this are shown in the table on page 101, stated in terms of years and miles. For example, 3/36,000 means the warranty is good for 3 years or 36,000 miles, whichever comes first. Since warranty policies can change, you should check the current specifics for the makes you're considering.

The most important warranty, by far, is the basic bumper-to-bumper coverage. For most people, it doesn't make sense to accept below-average basic coverage from an automaker, even in return for superior powertrain coverage.

In the past, powertrain warranties covered most of the major problems

WARRANTIES

Manufacturer	Basic Warranty	Powertrain Warranty	Rust-through Warranty
Acura	4/50,000	4/50,000	5/unlimited
Audi	3/50,000	3/50,000	10/unlimited
BMW	4/50,000	4/50,000	6/unlimited
Buick	3/36,000	3/36,000	6/100,000
Cadillac	4/50,000	4/50,000	6/100,000
Chevrolet	3/ 36,000	3/36,000	6/100,000
Chrysler	3/36,000	3/36,000	7/100,000
Dodge	3/36,000	3/36,000	7/100,000
Eagle	3/36,000	3/36,000	7/100,000
Ford	3/36,000	3/36,000	5/unlimited
Geo	3/36,000	3/36,000	6/100,000
Honda	3/36,000	3/36,000	5/unlimited
Hyundai	3/36,000	5/60,000	5/100,000
Infiniti	4/60,000	6/70,000	7/unlimited
Isuzu	3/50,000	5/60,000	6/100,000
Jaguar	4/50,000	4/50,000	6/unlimited
Kia	3/36,000	5/60,000	3/50,000
Land Rover	3/42,000	3/42,000	6/unlimited
Lexus	4/50,000	6/70,000	6/unlimited
Lincoln	4/50,000	4/50,000	6/100,000
Mazda	3/50,000	3/50,000	5/unlimited
Mercedes-Benz	4/50,000	4/50,000	4/50,000
Mercury	3/36,000	3/36,000	5/unlimited
Mitsubishi	3/36,000	5/60,000	7/100,000
Nissan	3/36,000	5/60,000	5/unlimited
Oldsmobile	3/36,000	3/36,000	6/100,000
Oldsmobile Aurora	4/50,000	4/50,000	6/100,000
Plymouth	3/36,000	3/36,000	7/100,000
Pontiac	3/36,000	3/36,000	6/100,000
Porsche	2/unlimited	2/unlimited	10/unlimited
Saab	4/50,000	4/50,000	6/unlimited
Saturn	3/36,000	3/36,000	6/100,000
Subaru	3/36,000	5/60,000	5/unlimited
Suzuki	3/36,000	3/36,000	3/unlimited
Toyota	3/36,000	5/60,000	5/unlimited
Volkswagen	2/24,000	10/100,000	6/unlimited
Volvo	4/50,000	4/50,000	8/unlimited

encountered after the original warranty expired because the only really expensive repair bills came from powertrain problems.

Today's automobiles, however, are loaded with complicated new systems that have nothing to do with the things that make the car go. Electronic instrument panels with all kinds of gadgets. Power equipment options. Antilock braking systems. Cruise control. Airbags. Sophisticated steering and suspension systems.

Diagnosing and fixing problems with these systems is more difficult and expensive than it was with their predecessors. And when they need fixing after the basic warranty period, it's your money that's on the line.

Worth noting: Several import makes have competitive basic warranties and separate powertrain warranties extending beyond the bumper-to-bumper coverage. This makes their warranties somewhat better, overall, than any domestic company's.

With most major manufacturers now at or near parity on basic warranty coverage, the decision on whether to buy an extended warranty contract will depend on how long you'll keep the vehicle and how far you'll drive it.

THIS CAN BE EXPENSIVE OVERINSURANCE

Remember, these extended warranties don't kick in until the basic coverage expires. If you buy a car with an initial factory warranty of 36 months or 36,000 miles, your extension coverage doesn't begin until either mile number 36,001 or the first day of month 37.

Will you keep the car that long and/or drive it that far? If you will, how much longer and farther do you think you'll own and drive it? It you're not sure, it may be better to put $500 aside as self-insurance against a big-bucks repair bill. (This alternative may be very attractive if you're buying a Toyota or Nissan product that comes with an extended powertrain warranty.) But if you're planning to drive the car until the wheels fall off, an extended warranty can be a wise investment.

Note that you probably don't have to make this decision when you buy the car. In most cases, you may purchase this contract anytime within the first 12 months or 12,000 miles. You're likely to buy it more cheaply, however, as part of the initial vehicle purchase, when you'll have more negotiating leverage. When you return to buy it later, they'll know it's something you really want and try to get top dollar for it.

FOUR IMPORTANT SUGGESTIONS FOR CONTRACT BUYERS

1. *Buy only a factory-backed warranty,* not one that's backed only by a third party. In recent years, several third-party underwriters have gone bankrupt. Many unwary consumers were left holding worthless contracts that neither the factories nor the dealers would honor.

2. *Read the fine print.* Understand which parts are not covered, whether there's a deductible charge per repair, whether the contract is transferable if you sell the car, and whether you'll get any money back if you cancel.

3. *The price is as negotiable as the price of the car.* Salesmen will tell you that an expensive post-warranty repair could cost you over $2,000, making this $1,000+ "insurance policy" a good investment. What they won't tell you is that this $1,000+ extended coverage contract costs them only $200 to $500.

This is one of the highest-margin items any car store sells. If you want it, offer *half* the asking price, and don't pay more than *two thirds.* Many dealers today would rather sell it and make $200 than not sell it and make nothing.

4. *Use it or lose it.* With both the initial bumper-to-bumper factory coverage and the extended protection, why have it if you don't use it? This question is especially relevant as you approach the end of the coverage periods.

During the last month or the last 1,000 miles of coverage, ask your dealer's service department to go over the car thoroughly to determine whether any major problems are on the horizon. Request that they do something now about these problems, while your car is still under warranty. A good service operation will be glad to do this for a regular customer.

19

*Two roads diverged in a
wood, and I—
I took the one less traveled by,
And that has made all the
difference.*

—Robert Frost,
The Road Not Taken

Choosing

Your Dealer

Finalists

Now it's time to pick the dealers you'll visit for serious price negotiations on your finalist vehicles. Given what we've told you so
far, this may seem as if we're throwing you a curve ball. We're
not; this is simply one more aspect of smart buying.

*The dealer you want to buy from will not necessarily be the one who'll give
you the best price, but the one who'll give you the best service.*

Your dealer finalists should be those that satisfy two key requirements:

1. They're geographically desirable, reasonably close to either your home or workplace.

2. They've got service departments with above-average track records.

The convenience factor is obvious. The last thing you need is a 40-mile round trip to have your car serviced regularly. The "service-over-price" factor is less obvious. We are not suggesting that you pay a hefty premium to buy from the dealer who will service your vehicle; if his price is a lot higher, buy somewhere else. (You might even say to him, "I plan to have the car serviced here, and I'd like to buy it here, but I'm not going to pay a big penalty to do that.") But there are advantages to buying where you'll have an ongoing relationship, and they may justify paying a modest premium in the price of the car.

You need a good ongoing relationship with a dealer's service department if you're going to get your money's worth from the second most expensive purchase of your life, the machine you count on daily to take you where you need to go. With the right dealer and the right service department, you can get so much more than your money's worth that the $100 to $200 you might save buying the car somewhere else will look like very small change—especially when you need warranty work.

According to the National Automobile Dealers Association (NADA), parts and service represent roughly 15 percent of the average dealership's total sales, but account for over 80 percent of total profits! If parts and service is the golden goose, you can bet that dealers are going to protect that goose any way they can to maximize their profits.

As you probably know, any franchised dealer will perform repairs on your car that are covered by warranty. But most people don't know that dealers make less profit on factory-paid warranty repairs than on regular, customer-paid work. Here's how dealers typically are compensated for warranty work:

- First, while the factories might pay dealers the same hourly wage rate for warranty work that you pay for nonwarranty work, they typically set specific time limits for almost every type of repair and won't compensate dealers for additional time spent. For many legitimate reasons, including difficulty in pinpointing problems quickly, the time spent can exceed the time allowed, and dealers frequently end up "eating" a lot of that unreimbursed time.

- Second, and probably more important, the manufacturers control the dealer's markup on warranty parts, thus limiting a major profit opportunity. You may assume that the retail markup on parts that you pay for ranges from 60 percent to 100 percent, depending on the part and the dealer. But the domestic and import automakers, which profit substantially by selling the dealer those same parts, pay him a much smaller wholesale markup on those used in warranty work—typically 40 to 45 percent. (It used to be only 30 percent.)

But wait, there's more!

• The paperwork blizzard required of dealers to document and claim reimbursement for warranty repairs is a costly nightmare. (If you've ever signed off on warranty work, you know.) And, of course, the speed of factory reimbursement doesn't compare with the instant payment received from customers for nonwarranty work.

• Finally, to add insult to injury, many manufacturers require that dealers save the replaced parts so that they can check them later, if they wish, to ensure that those parts did, indeed, warrant replacing.

You don't need to be a rocket scientist to understand why no service manager in his right mind would want to load his shop on any given day with warranty work, especially for customers who bought their cars somewhere else.

ARE THERE TWO CLASSES OF OWNERSHIP?

Whenever one dealer has a better service operation than others selling the same make, the word gets around. People start using that better service facility more, especially when their factory warranties have expired and they're spending their own money. (That's why there are a dozen cars in line at 7 a.m. at some dealerships and only two or three customers at the same-make dealership three miles down the road.)

So what does the manager of that busy first-class service operation do when you call to schedule warranty work on a car you bought somewhere else?

• First, he checks his schedule. If it's crowded, he may put you off to a slow day later in the week, when he'd rather have warranty work than no work. (But he'd probably find a way to squeeze in a regular customer.)

• Perhaps, if he takes you, he might tell you he's not sure he can get it out today. (You could end up at the end of the line if enough regular customers come in.) And you may get one of those phone calls saying, "We can't finish the job today because we need to send out for a part."

But more important, long-term, is what he doesn't do, which is go out of his way to do anything special for you. He'll follow the letter of the law, but he probably won't bend it in your favor, as he might for regulars.

To illustrate, let's look at some things a good service operation can do to keep its regular customers happy.

CREATIVE RULE-BENDING

Has this ever happened to you? You take your car in for regular service and learn when you pick it up that they've fixed something important, something that you didn't even know was broken. Since this expensive work is covered by your warranty, you're pleased that the service department was so thorough.

You'll probably be surprised to learn that there's a reasonable chance that they didn't make that repair to your car, they made it to the car of another good customer whose warranty, perhaps, had recently expired. They simply charged the factory paperwork to your (in-warranty) car. Neither you nor the other customer knew this, but you both drove home happy.

The manufacturers' service people will never admit that they condone this action, but they want happy customers, too. A few bad dealer service operations can affect their company's overall consumer satisfaction ratings, which, in turn, can affect sales. Common sense says they're likely to look the other way when the rules get bent occasionally by a dealer who keeps his customers happy.

Here's another example of how a good service operation can make life simpler for a valued customer. Have you ever had a car perform badly all day, but when you took it to the dealer it ran beautifully, and their computer analyzer said all the parts were fine?

You had "an intermittent problem," which is often the lead-in to a terminal problem, but because the computer said the part was okay, the dealer couldn't replace it under warranty. (Remember, the factories want them to save the replaced parts so they can check their condition and refuse payment if they still work.)

A first-class service department may handle this more creatively. They don't want customers' problems to reappear after they've declared their vehicles fixed. They've seen this complaint before, and they know which part is causing the problem. They decide to replace it now, despite what the computer says. To eliminate any potential reimbursement problem, they'll hook up that used part to their Godzilla Electric Chair to guarantee that it'll be a dead soldier, if and when the manufacturer tests it.

We're not saying these things are done routinely every day. But they are done, and they're more likely to be done for the most valued customers. And that's why, if you have your car serviced where you bought it, it's a good idea to leave the dealer's license plate frame on the car as a reminder to his service people that you're one of them.

Incidentally, a good service department doesn't necessarily have to bend the rules to accomplish small miracles for you. Many times they'll simply call the manufacturer's regional service manager and ask for special favors for good customers. And the factory people are more likely to grant favors to a service operation that causes them fewer problems.

THE PERVASIVE POWER OF THE CSI

As everyone with a TV set must know by now, CSI stands for Customer Satisfaction Index. In the competitive market they face today, both the manufacturers and their dealers are in the CSI business, not the automobile business. CSI scores are important on several levels:

• On one level, J. D. Power and Associates' CSI data is publicized nationally, providing an important halo for the auto makes that score well. The leaders celebrate their performance in advertising, and consumers are influenced positively.

• On another level, recognizing the critical importance of satisfied customers, the manufacturers are conducting regular in-depth research among their own buyers to establish CSI ratings for each individual dealership. This helps them identify rotten apples that might spoil the whole crop.

It also gives them a basis for rewarding top performers. Many automakers base dealer bonus payments on customer satisfaction as well as sales. For example, Chrysler has a dealer cash incentive system in which the payments are based on a combination of sales performance and consumer satisfaction ratings. (This is what prompted former chairman Lee Iacocca to quip, "It seems a helluva note in life that we must pay a dealer to be nice to his customers.")

Individual dealer CSI scores also provide a rationale for allocating scarce product. For example, in order to qualify to sell Dodge's expensive, limited-volume Viper sports car, dealers were required to have a minimum CSI score on Chrysler's internal rating scale.

• Finally, a dealer's CSI in his current stores is a key factor in determining whether he'll be chosen by another manufacturer when it's expanding its dealer base.

Many dealers today are mega-dealers who own several different franchises. For example, of the more than 500 Mitsubishi dealers, about 20 percent also have Chevrolet franchises, 15 percent Toyota, 15 percent Nissan, 14 percent Hyundai, 14 percent Oldsmobile, 14 percent Honda and 13 percent Ford. The average Mitsubishi dealer owns 2.7 franchises. And only the ones with above-average CSI scores are likely to get additional makes to sell.

The Great CSI Scores Are Built on Service, Not Sales

Once you drive that car home, your longer-term impressions of satisfaction with the selling dealer will reflect how well a dealer's service operation treats you and your expensive baby. Smart dealers understand that "price may bring 'em in, but service brings 'em back." These dealers work harder than others to keep customers happy, and that extra effort helps keep their overall CSI scores among the leaders. These are the kinds of dealers you want.

Assuming you're sold on this point of view, it's time to narrow your choices.

CHOOSING YOUR FINALISTS

You can learn something useful from the dealership experiences of friends and neighbors driving the same make. But you'll gain the most insight by doing your own research, relatively painlessly, over the phone.

☎ Reaching Out Again

• Start by making a list of geographically acceptable dealers. Call each and ask for the name of the service manager.

• Then call those managers, one by one, and have a little truth session. Tell him your name. Say you're planning to buy that make of car or truck in the next couple of weeks, and that you're trying to pick the right dealer. Tell him you think that several dealers are going to be pretty close to each other on price. But even if they're not, in the final analysis, the quality of the service department will be more important to you in the long run than saving a few hundred dollars up front, and you'd like to talk to him for a couple of minutes about his service operation.

He will like this attitude because it places the focus where he thinks it should be. It also affirms his importance in the dealership. While he runs his own show (reporting to the dealer's general manager) and produces the bulk of the dealership's profit, he probably doesn't get the respect he deserves. (Most dealer principals are sales types, as are their general managers.)

Specific Areas to Probe

• First, ask how long he's been there, and where else he's worked. (If he's just arrived, how long was the previous manager there?)

• Then, acknowledging his significant experience, ask him what he thinks may be better about his service operation than some of his same-make competitors. This will give him an open field, so to speak, and he should have some substantive things to say. If he's got a good story to tell, you may hear about how well equipped his shop is, the factory training his people get regularly, his attitude toward customers and even the dealership's overall CSI.

• If you don't hear these things, either he's shy and inarticulate or he's got no great story to tell. Give him the benefit of the doubt, and ask a few more detailed questions.

✔ **Ask about the dealership's overall CSI score, and specifically, how it stacks up against other same-make dealers in the same factory sales zone.** This is something he has to know about, given its importance to the dealer and his department's key role in making sure it's favorable. If his CSI is above average, he should be glad to tell you about it. If he hedges or says he's not sure, it's probably below average. Ask if he'd show you the report if you came in to see him. You want to buy where the CSI is at least average or better, compared to other stores in the same factory sales area.

✔ **Ask how well equiped his shop is.** Does he have to send cars out for many operations? For example, does he have wheel alignment and wheel balancing equipment? A brake lathe to turn drums (for drum brakes) and rotors (for disc brakes)?

✔ **Has the dealership won any recent factory awards for service**

excellence? Do his people regularly get to go to factory training sessions (or is the boss too tight to send them)?

✔ **Does the dealer offer a courtesy shuttle service** to take customers to work or home after they drop off a car? (Many do, but few will also pick you up to return later.) Are there loaner cars or low-cost rentals? And are the service department's hours convenient for you?

Obviously, what you want to hear is that the CSI is above average for the sales zone, the service manager's job there is not a revolving door, the shop is well equipped, it wins factory excellence awards frequently, the mechanics attend factory training courses regularly, and he'd be glad to give you a shop tour, if you'd like.

After two unsuccessful attempts, beware of service managers who don't return your calls. If you have trouble getting them for a five-minute phone conversation, you may assume their customers have the same problem.

The Envelope, Please . . .

All service departments are not created equal, and you'll learn a lot from this relatively painless exercise. You should be able to pick two or three finalist dealerships near home or work. You may even come away with a sense of which dealer you'd like to buy from.

None of this means you're going to be any less disciplined in negotiating price! You're still going to work those sales operations for a minimum-profit deal. You may even use price quotes from car stores you'd never consider buying from to get concessions from your finalists. Whatever deal you strike, you'll be happier buying from the right dealer because your ongoing relationship is more likely to be a good one.

20

People who have no weakness are terrible; there is no way of taking advantage of them.

—Anatole France

Showtime!

You've done all your homework. You've decided either to sell your old car yourself at retail or sell it to a dealer at wholesale, and you've learned its true wholesale value. You've decided how much you can spend, and you've researched financing alternatives. You've taken your test drives and chosen your vehicle and dealer finalists. You've got your worksheets showing dealer invoice costs, current consumer and dealer incentives, dealer holdback (if any) and carryover allowance (for a model-year leftover).

Most important, you've got at least one alternative vehicle that's an acceptable option to your first choice, and a couple of colors you'd be happy with for each.

You're ready for the games salesmen play and the back-end add-ons they'll try to sell. You've decided whether you're a candidate for an extended warranty contract. And you've timed your "talk turkey" visits for either the end of the month or the end of a juicy dealer incentive program.

You've reviewed Chapter 4 (Psychology 101, Anatomy 101 and Reality 101) and Chapter 7 (Divide and Conquer). You've got the knowledge and the right attitude, and you're going to be a very disciplined shopper. You're just about ready.

THE GAME PLAN

Let's review what you're going to accomplish:

1. You'll visit at least three dealer finalists to negotiate a slim-profit price, using your knowledge to get a better deal than the 99.9 percent of buyers who don't have this knowledge. The car stores will understand they're competing against each other for your money, not against you. And you'll keep the price negotiation completely separate from any discussion of selling your old car or financing the new one.

However you plan to finance the vehicle, it's a good idea at the outset to give the impression that you've got an open mind about financing through the dealership, if the terms are attractive. Chances are, you'll negotiate a better purchase price if they think they have a shot at the financing profit; if they know in advance that you'll finance somewhere else or pay cash, they may hold out for a higher-profit deal. (The same thinking applies to your potential trade-in. Even if you've decided to sell it yourself, let them think initially that you'd consider selling it to them.)

2. After establishing the new-car price, you may open the discussion of financing, telling the salesman you'd like to know what the dealer or the factory has to offer so that you can compare it with other options.

3. At that time you may also open the discussion of your old car, saying that you might want to sell it to a dealer, depending on the price, and asking how much they'd pay for it. You'll also make it clear that you know what your vehicle is worth at wholesale, and that you don't plan to leave any money on the table.

WHAT SHOULD YOUR TARGET PRICE
BE FOR THE NEW CAR?

In a word, low. The automobile market is the most competitive environment in retailing, mainly because there are twice as many makes, models and dealers as any civilized society needs. Use that fact to your advantage by playing those makes, models and dealers off against each other to get what you want: the lowest price.

Remember the key insight we've gained from the thousands of customers who have used the Fighting Chance information service: *Most dealers agree to several slim-profit deals each month with customers who have done their homework and know how to use it.*

Dealers are eager to move their inventory. They've got acres of vehicles, each costing them $75 to $150 a month in floor plan interest. They want those autos in your garage and in their service bays, where they make the real profits. Selling one more car this month and making a modest profit always beats not selling it and making those interest payments again.

Think of yourself as the incremental sale, from the dealer's perspective. Assume that they are always dealing—either because sales are down and they want to move them up, or because sales are up and they want to keep them up. And don't be bashful about presenting lowball offers. Remember that you can always go back and offer more, but you can't go back and offer less.

Having said this, we should add that it is appropriate for a dealer to make a fair profit when he sells you a product worth six months' wages for the average household. You just don't want the profit on your deal to finance his next round-the-world cruise. And of course, his definition of "fair" may differ substantially from yours.

Here are some general target price guidelines for cars in good supply, based on the feedback we've received on actual transaction prices from Fighting Chance customers:

• For cars with suggested retail prices up to about $25,000, you can feel good about prices in the range of $300 to $700 over the dealer invoice price. It doesn't seem to matter whether the car is priced at $12,500 or $25,000; transaction prices for people who have done their homework and are willing to walk out of the showroom once or twice seem to fall in this general range. Some tough negotiators will beat this range on the low end, depending on how desperate the dealer is to sell. Others may pay a little more on the high end, depending on how anxious they are to buy.

- For vehicles with suggested retail prices from $25,000 to $40,000, the range of transaction prices among knowledgeable customers is $500 to $900 over dealer invoice on the lower end of the price spectrum and $1,000 to $1,500 over invoice on the higher end. Again, some may do a little better and others a little worse, but you can feel that you've done pretty well anywhere in these ranges.

- For cars with sticker prices from $40,000 to $60,000, the target range is $1,500 to $3,000 over the dealer invoice price. We regularly get reports of customers paying $2,000 to $3,000 over invoice for cars with MSRPs of $50,000+ that have about a $10,000 profit built into the sticker price.

- The most expensive high-end luxury cars, with sticker prices above $60,000, can be relatively easy to deal on. Dealers don't want to inventory many of them, but they like to have one or two in the showroom as image builders for the dealership. Most dealers want to move those cars regularly. Often a few thousand dollars profit will motivate them to sell, even if there's a $15,000 to $20,000 profit built into the sticker price. Selling the same car several times a year, so to speak, gives the dealer more overall profit than waiting for the occasional rare deal that delivers the maximum profit for a single sale. He knows he's in a competitive business, even at the highest end.

In all cases, we've assumed the dealer will earn his factory holdback dollars in addition to the profit ranges outlined above. A dealer will almost never share his holdback with you; he counts on it to pay some of his overhead. But you will strengthen your bargaining position by reminding him that you know about it and mentioning the dollar amount, making it more difficult for him to plead poverty when you offer him a slim-profit deal. (One Fighting Chance customer called a Volvo dealer and asked whether he'd like to sell a car today and make a $1,000 profit—his offer of $200 over invoice plus the $800 holdback he'd get from Volvo—and the dealer accepted the offer.)

When one dealer has to obtain the car you want from another dealer, the holdback profit typically remains with the original dealer. But don't let them use this fact as an excuse for a higher selling price. Dealers regularly trade cars back and forth; it helps all of them operate with lower inventories. Each dealer wins some and loses some, but the trades tend to even out over a period of several months.

The price range guidelines above apply to all cars, domestics and imports. Import franchises used to be much tougher to deal with, but times have changed. Today even Honda dealers run ads about prices "$100 over invoice." The Honda Accord is one of the best-selling cars in the United States, and the best-selling cars in any country are not in short supply. Anyone who isn't buying a Honda or any other import make for well under MSRP isn't negotiating a realistic price in today's market. If an import dealer won't talk price, move down the road to one who will. He's waiting for you, with a lot full of unsold cars.

If there's a factory-to-dealer incentive program on the car you want, you should end up with all of it because you're paying for all of it. If he'd sell you the car for, say, $500 over invoice if there were no incentive, he would settle for the same profit with customers who know about the factory-to-dealer cash. Make him an offer that starts with the invoice price, subtracts the entire incentive, then adds back an appropriate profit. If one dealer won't cooperate, take your business to another who will. In a market with several competing dealers, they shouldn't be hard to find.

Direct customer rebates should be kept out of the price negotiation. They are your entitlement, almost always paid entirely by the factory. You'll use them as part of your payment after the price is settled. (Typically, you'll sign a document that authorizes the automaker to credit your rebate to the dealer's account.)

If you're shopping for a model-year leftover of a Ford or GM vehicle, you should request that the entire factory carryover allowance (5 percent of MSRP) be deducted from the price you pay. That car's value dropped like a rock the day the new models hit the dealer's lot, and 5 percent of the sticker price doesn't begin to cover the loss.

What should you pay for a demo, a car that's been used at the dealership but never purchased by an individual? As a general rule, we don't think you should buy a demo unless you can save thousands of dollars, compared to the price you'd negotiate for an unused version of the same vehicle. One issue to consider is warranty coverage. Frequently these demos have been driven 5,000 to 10,000 miles. If the car's original bumper-to-bumper warranty is 3 years/36,000 miles and you drive 13,000 miles a year, you'll run out of basic warranty coverage after just two years if you buy a demo with 10,000 miles on the odometer. A dealer may tell you that coverage starts the day you buy the car, which is true for time, but the warranty's mileage limitation almost always applies. Remember, 3/36,000 coverage means 3 years *or* 36,000 miles, *whichever comes first*. If you have any doubts, contact the manufacturer before you sign anything. (One solution for this problem: Ask the dealer to include the manufacturer's extended warranty in the deal.)

If a demo's mileage isn't too high, the issue will be whether the price is low enough. Assuming you can buy a brand-new version for $500 over invoice, how much below that is low enough? There is no easy answer. We wouldn't trade even 3,000 or 4,000 warranty miles just to save another $1,000. Most demos are sold relatively late in the model year and have depreciated significantly. Yet the dealer usually can't sell them for a figure low enough to cover that depreciation. In essence, you'll be buying a used car, which loses 20 to 30 percent of its value as a one-year-old, but paying too close to a new-car price. And when you sell it to the next owner, you'll get less because of those extra miles on the odometer. For all of these reasons, it would take savings of a few thousand dollars to make a demo purchase attractive to us.

ARE THERE VEHICLES ON WHICH YOU CAN'T DEAL?

Yes. You won't get much of a price break on any car when the demand exceeds the supply. The most common example is a hot-selling new model in the first few months after its introduction. And if you must have the only teal green Accord coupe within five hundred square miles, it'll cost a lot more than those blue ones lined up on every dealer's lot.

As we noted in Chapter 17, frequently there are one or two vehicles in short supply because they have become popular almost overnight and automakers can't add production capacity quickly enough to meet demand. In that situation, you may have to take a number, get in line and pay a lot more than you'd like. You should consider postponing your purchase or placing a factory order. If you can't do either, try calling around in neighboring markets to find a high-volume dealer. Remember, product allocations are based primarily on past sales performance. A dealer who sells just one or two a month gets only one or two a month, and he's going to hold out for the maximum profit on a scarce vehicle. But other dealers who sell and receive 20 or 30 a month may be much more flexible on pricing, if only to move more units and ensure their future supply.

There used to be several makes noted for holding firm on price, but they have become a vanishing breed. The European luxury-car dealers would have liked to play the game by the old rules indefinitely, but the Japanese invasion of their high-end turf has changed their attitude, and they are dealing.

The bottom line is that you should make aggressively low offers to just about any dealer today. If it's the end of the month and the cars are sitting there, he just might bite. Remember, you can always decide to pay more later.

THE OTHER CAVEAT: COMPETITIVE GEOGRAPHY

There's another factor that can severely restrict your ability to negotiate a favorable price: the number of dealers for a given make within competitive geography. If you live in a smaller market and there's only one dealer for the car you want within a reasonable driving radius, he's got real pricing leverage. Our advice: Shop by phone or fax with the sales managers at dealerships in the nearest major market, then ask the local dealer if he's really going to force you to leave town to buy the car for a reasonable price. Chances are, you'll reach a compromise price that will keep the business in your town, where you'd both like it to be.

GM's Saturn is a special case, where price competition doesn't exist because each dealer has been given an exclusive sales territory. Eventually, there may be several Saturn stores in your town, but they're all likely to be owned by the same person. And he's not going to compete with himself on price. In our view, Saturn has traded a selling system that takes advantage of some people for one that takes advantage of everyone. (See Chapter 12.)

CREATIVE SNOOPING FOR THE CAR YOU WANT

Before you begin serious price negotiations, it would be helpful to know whether any dealers in town already have the vehicle you want, outfitted to your specifications. Everything else being equal, you'll have more leverage if they already own it, are paying inventory carrying charges on it, and will get the holdback profit when it's sold. You can then call or walk in and say that they've got a car you're prepared to drive home today if the price is right.

To gather this intelligence without being pounced upon by a car salesman, get up early some morning—early enough to be walking around the lots between 7:00 and 8:00 a.m. The service department may be open, but you're unlikely to see salesmen before 9:00 a.m. (On a Sunday, you won't see anyone except perhaps the security guard at that hour.) If anyone asks what you're doing, tell them you're just fantasizing about your next birthday present.

CURTAIN TIME!

Now we're going to take you through a hypothetical negotiating session. Of course, we can't script a single approach that will apply to all situations, but this example illustrates how you can use your strong base of knowledge in a very disciplined way to achieve the result you want. Think of it as a cat-and-mouse game, with you as the cat. You've got all the tools you need to win, and dealing from strength can actually be fun.

"The Hammer, Wrapped in Velvet"

Start by visiting the dealer you'd most like to buy from, so that you can avoid wasting time with others if you get the price you want. Walk into the showroom with your worksheet pad under your arm. A salesman will greet you. (You're his "up.") He will not be happy to see your pad. If he comments on it, tell him you've got a terrible memory and might want to refer to some notes.

A note of caution: If you are female and are greeted by a saleswoman, don't assume that's a stroke of good fortune. In the research discussed in Chapter 2, dealerships seemed to steer testers to salespeople of their own gender and race, who proceeded to offer them worse deals than other testers received from people of a different gender and race. Would a nice saleswoman try to take advantage of you? You can bet on it. No matter how nice she may seem, she is assuming that you will trust her, and that your trust will lead to a higher-profit deal.

From the start, you should be friendly but quite confident, disciplined and firm. You are definitely someone who knows what you want, and knows a lot about what you want. (He'll quickly learn that you know more than 99.9 percent of the people who walk through the door.)

You're knowledgeable, but you're not going to be cocky about it. What you are going to be is very straightforward. And you are always going to act like someone who is going to buy a car.

Smile and introduce yourself. Then tell him that you're definitely going to buy a car in the next week or so, you've taken test drives and know exactly what you want, you're shopping several dealers and you're going to buy where you get the best price. Then add that a friend wants to buy your old car, but you're not sure that's a good idea. Tell him you've checked out some financing alternatives, but haven't made a decision. And say that you'll be happy to discuss selling your old car to them, and to consider the dealership's financing options, but not until you've settled on the price of the new vehicle.

As an overall tactical objective, you want to be the one asking the questions, defining the key issues that need to be resolved and moving the discussion in a straight line toward a resolution. That way the pressure will be on the salesman to respond to your moves, making it difficult for him to get and keep control of the sales situation.

For example, when he begins asking personal questions about your job or marital status, it's perfectly appropriate to say, "Please don't take this the wrong way, but I know your time is valuable, and if it's okay with you I'd rather get into a discussion about the car. I already know I can qualify for financing; the question is whether we can agree on a price." If he hasn't invited you to sit in an office by this time, suggest that you go to one to discuss a possible deal in more detail.

When you get there, tell him nicely (perhaps with a little self-conscious smile, but maintaining good eye contact) that you know the auto business is supercompetitive today, and that although that makes it tougher for him you plan to take advantage of that competition, just as he would if he were you.

Then tell him the things he will least like to hear: that you've done your homework, you know the dealer invoice price, you're aware of any consumer rebates or factory-to-dealer cash offers in effect, and you've got a feel for realistic transaction prices among knowledgeable buyers. Add that you're not going to try to beat him out of every dollar, you expect him to make a profit on the sale, but that he's not going to finance his next Hawaiian vacation on your deal. Say that if he wants to sell you a car and make a reasonable profit, you'll be an easy customer to close quickly. But that if they want to play their good cop/bad cop, back-and-forth game, you're not going to let them waste your time, and you won't waste theirs. *Then bite your tongue and wait for a response.* The pressure will be on him, not on you.

Remember, you're saying this very calmly, as a really nice person who is also a very knowledgeable shopper they aren't going to be able to fool.

What You've Already Accomplished

You've won the first skirmish with this straight-ahead, no-baloney approach, and you've neutralized his major weapon. He can't do what he does with most prospects at this stage—find their hot button (whether they're payment buyers or trade-in allowance buyers, etc.) and move to exploit it.

You've defined the turf on which the battle will be fought: simple cash price. You've also put all the key issues on the table early in the game, making it difficult for him to waste your time bobbing and weaving around them. You are going to learn, reasonably quickly, whether these people want to sell you a car and get on to the next customer or work hard to make you a victim of Life's 80/20 Rule—the one that says 80 percent of the profits come from 20 percent of the buyers.

TAKING CONTROL

At this point the salesman may continue to work with you himself, or he may have been told to pass the most knowledgeable customers along to his sales manager. They may even spirit you away to another part of the office, so that you won't contaminate their other customers.

Whether you're dealing with the original salesman or with someone new, your next move should be to take out your worksheet, telling him that the best figure to start with is the dealer invoice price. By now he's probably classified you as a tough customer, which is fine. (It's wrapped in velvet, but your hammer is there.) *Remember that it's much easier for you to find another dealer than for him to find another real prospect.* As long as you act like someone who's going to buy somewhere soon, he'll keep the discussion alive. To shorten the agony for both of you, you should be prepared to make an opening offer, one that's somewhat below what you're really willing to pay for the car. Here's an approach to moving the dialogue along:

Let's assume there's a current $400 to $800 factory-to-dealer incentive program on your vehicle. For openers, you should start with the total dealer invoice price (including the cost of all optional equipment and the destination charge), subtract the entire $800 factory-to-dealer cash payment, then add back a reasonable profit number. For example, if the vehicle's sticker price is $25,000 or less and you're willing to give them a profit of $500, leave yourself some negotiating room by offering them, say, $250 in your opening bid. Remind him that any direct consumer rebate doesn't figure into this offer, that it will simply be part of your cash payment after you settle on a price.

Here's where you'll use your knowledge of holdback. While holdback isn't something most folks can extract from even the most desperate dealer, it can be used artfully in this game. Just before you end your opening-offer speech, you'll point to the dealer holdback line on your worksheet and tell him you know they'll get another $400 in holdback profit from your deal, making a total profit of $650. *Then bite your tongue and wait for a response.* (In this cat-and-mouse game, the next one who talks loses. Make sure it's the mouse.)

According to our feedback from Fighting Chance customers, most dealers are going to treat you in a straightforward manner from this point onward. They may not be delighted to hear what you know, but they do want to sell you a car. A very small number may actually kick you out of the store, but that's fine; you'll have uncovered their true colors without wasting half a day enduring their good cop/bad cop selling system. (Remember, you don't know where the bone is until you hit it. You can always call later and offer them more.)

Usually they won't accept your opening offer, whatever it is. If they did, they'd worry that you'd have buyer's remorse, wondering if you'd offered too much. You might even get cold feet, refuse to sign the deal and go down the street to another car store to see if they'd take less. So always expect them to "bump" your offer. Here are some of the responses you can expect to encounter:

• He might say first that there's no way they can sell that car for anything like the price you offered. Your response should be that if that's the case, all he has to do is give you a firm "no," and you'll go somewhere else. (Be gathering your things, getting ready to walk out as you're saying this. He will not tell you to go.)

• Since he knows you've been shopping elsewhere, he might ask what price the other guys have quoted, or what price he has to beat. Your response, with a smile: "The only price you need to match if you want to sell me a car is the one in my offer." (It's never a good idea to tell any salesman the prices other salesmen quote.)

• He also might tell you to go out and shop around for the best price, then come back and he'll beat it. You'll say, "I'm sorry, I'm not going to spend a month playing games with car dealers. I am going to buy a car from some dealer within the next week. But if we can't move the discussion along to a final price on this visit, I won't be back to do it later." If he refuses, you should leave.

• He may say that your invoice cost numbers are wrong. Your response will be to call his bluff, nicely, by asking him to take out his factory invoice so you can compare the numbers and see where they differ. Tell him you'd be glad to go out to the lot to compare your suggested retail prices with those on the Monroney sticker on the car, and that you expect the MSRP numbers to match exactly. Add that when they do, you'll both know that your invoice numbers are right on the money. Say that if he's going to tell you that the automaker raised the price to the dealer without passing any of the increase along to the customer, you're going to have a problem believing anything he says. (Note, however, that most dealers add an advertising charge to their version of the invoice price, though it is not included on the manufacturer's sticker. This is a legitimate expense, discussed later in the chapter.)

• If you're still with the original salesman, he probably doesn't have the authority to finalize a deal. Which means he's got to take your offer to his boss. As he leaves—without the hostage deposit check you refuse to write—tell him nicely that you don't know how his store operates, but you're not going to wait there long for him to return. If he's not back in about five minutes, you'll leave. Also say, with due respect for his position, that if he's not someone whom you can bargain with directly to a final purchase price, without passing a lot of messages back and forth, he should bring the decision maker with him when he comes back.

Don't just sit there while he's gone. To strengthen your psychological advantage, wander around the lot, so that he'll have to look for you when he returns. That'll make him worry that you might leave, and it'll ensure that he won't be gone long, "negotiating for you." (Remember, if he doesn't sell cars, he doesn't eat. He needs you.)

- His boss is likely to say that they can't sell a car at that price without losing money; they've got more invested in floor plan interest payments than your offer allows in profit; they're not going to earn the maximum dealer incentive of $800 anyway; and the bottom line is they need an additional $700 to even consider a deal.

Your response should be that you hope that's not his best price, because if it is he's not going to sell you a car. Take out your worksheet and let him look at it. Tell him that you're surprised that a big sales operation like his isn't at or near the maximum incentive payout two days from the end of the program, that dealers who seem to have less volume and inventory have said they were getting the full $800, and that you guess you ought to buy from one of them. Say that you'd expect him to be even more eager to sell you a car if he's below the target with only two days to go.

Then move the discussion along by adding $100 to your bid, offering him $350 plus the $400 holdback, for a total profit of $750. You already know what you should do next: *Bite your tongue and wait for a response.* If he comes down substantially and it's clear you can make a deal for your target price of $500 over invoice or less, then move to conclude the negotiation quickly and get on with your life. But if he moves by only $100 or so, he's probably expecting to start a series of concessions to see how much higher you'll go. When you refuse to budge, he'll ask, "Why don't we split the difference?"

Never, ever fall for this "generous" split-the-difference offer. Instead, this is where you'll get up and say very politely that it looks as if you aren't going to agree on a price today, that you've got some other stops to make, and that your phone number is 345-6789 if he has a change of heart later—99 percent of car salesmen do, 99 percent of the time. Then ask for his business card, thank him for his time and leave. You do have other stops to make. And he will be there later if you want him.

PREPARE FOR THE MATINEE

If that was a morning show and your emotional favorite didn't make an offer you couldn't refuse, plan a couple of afternoon performances at other dealer finalists. You'll be more comfortable in these shows, better prepared for the curve balls they'll throw because you've seen a few. By the end of the day, you'll have a good feel for the parameters of a possible deal and for the probable differences in price flexibility between dealers. Depending on the number of finalist dealers on your list, you may spend a second day completing these Round One visits.

As you review the bidding at the end of this round, factor in your feelings about where you really would like to buy. Where does that store stand on price? Whether it's on the high end or close to the leader, you'll have further discussions with the people there tomorrow.

☎ ROUND TWO

The next step can be handled best on the telephone. Call all of the players, the last ones you talked to in each store. Thank them again for their time, remind them that you're still planning to buy a new car in the next few days and that you're calling to see whether they've had a chance to think about your last offer. Your objective here is to get them down as low as they'll go for a live prospect, one they thought had got away.

They might ask, "What's the best price you've been offered?" Just say that it's well below their last offer. Whatever number they give you, tell them it's not your best offer but that you aren't going to make a decision until tomorrow, and they've got your phone number. Thank them again for their time and hang up.

Call your emotional favorite last. Start the conversation the same way. After his response, tell him that you'd really like to buy the car there, for reasons that go beyond price, but that you don't want to have to pay too dearly for the privilege. You live (or work) right nearby, and you hope he's not going to make you buy a car somewhere else.

Tell him he doesn't necessarily have to be the low bidder, but he's got to be in the ball park, and he's not quite there now. Emphasize again that you're ready to come down today and finalize the deal. *Then bite your tongue until he says something.*

If you've got two vehicles you'd be equally happy with, it's in your interest to take them both down to the wire. You might be surprised by one dealer's eleventh-hour concessions, especially near the end of a major factory-to-dealer incentive program.

Somewhere in this back-and-forth process, you'll find a deal and a dealer you can live with.

FINALIZING THE DEAL

Before leaving home, review Chapter 17 (Back-End Options: Just Say No). When you get to the dealership, make sure the car isn't loaded with dealer sticker items you don't want. If it is, demand that they throw them in free or find you a car without them.

Be alert at this stage for a host of little surprises, things salesmen "forget" to tell you about until they've got you so committed it would be a real hassle to walk away.

✔ For example, don't pay him a fee to process the documents. He can't sell anyone a car without processing documents. That's his cost of doing business, not yours.

✔ There's one surprise that virtually all dealers spring on customers these days—the local dealer association advertising charge. All manufacturers require their dealers to participate in the group advertising effort in their markets. The dealers form an advertising committee and decide how much each dealer will contribute per vehicle sold. This is typically 1–3 percent of the invoice price, depending on the number of dealers, the media costs in the market and how often the dealers want to run advertising. The charge is usually several hundred dollars per car, and dealers add it to their version of the invoice price. (On a Toyota dealer's invoice, for example, it might appear as TDA, or Toyota Dealer Association.) The manufacturers don't include this as part of their dealer invoice cost because the amount differs from market to market. In most cases where the dealer claims that your invoice price data is too low, this advertising charge is the main reason.

Is this a legitimate charge to the buyer? No, and yes. On one level, it's advertising, which is their expense, not yours. (And it worked, didn't it?) But consider this question: Don't the supermarket and the gas station charge you for their advertising? Of course they do; they just don't charge you separately for it when you pay the bill. If the manufacturers were brave enough to build this mandatory dealer charge into their invoice costs, there'd be nothing to debate. Since they aren't, we can understand why dealers pass it along.

Virtually all dealers are demanding that customers pay this group advertising expense (it's not for an individual store's advertising), and it is difficult to avoid. You really can't tell him that his competitors aren't charging for it, because that's unlikely to be true. If all dealers want to charge for advertising, you might try telling them that the one that doesn't charge will get the sale. Occasionally a dealer may not want to risk losing the sale over it. But you will probably have to pay it. Do it grudgingly, and try to use the concession to get one in return, like a set of deluxe carpet mats thrown in at no charge.

✔ If you want the extended warranty contract, make sure you understand what it covers and what the deductibles are, and confirm that it's guaranteed by the manufacturer. (Read all the fine print.) Then offer *half* of the asking price, and don't pay more than two thirds. Although you don't have to buy it when you purchase the car, they want to sell it then, and you'll never have as much bargaining leverage as you do when they think this could make or break the whole deal.

✔ Read every word ofthe sales agreement before you sign it. Make sure all the blanks are filled in. And be sure someone with proper authority signs it for the dealership before you do. (If the salesman's signature isn't binding, you don't have a firm deal.)

✔ This is the time to explore the potential appeal of the financing plans offered by the dealer. You've done your homework, so you've got a basis for comparison.

✔ This is also the time to say you're not sure it's smart to sell a used car to a friend. If the price were fair, you'd consider selling it to them. (Don't give them an asking price; make them give you a price first. And don't accompany them for the inspection show pantomime.) They'll take your car and come back with an offer, which you can counter based on the homework you've done on the car's true wholesale value. If they won't pay you that number, or something close to it, take it to one of those places that will. End of negotiations!

Unfortunately, buyers are not really wise on leasing right now. . . .If you are willing to pay $250 a month, I can make a lot of money on you. If you haven't compared me with other dealers on the details, I can probably really take advantage of you . . . if I were that kind of guy.

—General manager of a large import-make dealership (quoted in *Kiplinger's Personal Finance Magazine*)

The Leasing Alternative: Breaking the Language Barrier

R etail auto leasing has arrived, big-time. Pick up any paper. Half the car ads are pushing leases, and not just at the luxury end of the spectrum, where leased vehicles have traditionally accounted for over half of new-car sales. What's happening?

What's happening is that the prices of new cars have skyrocketed, and the automakers and their dealers have found leasing an effective way to combat monthly-payment creep. Leasing enables consumers to drive more car for the same monthly payment. Addressing the Consumer Bankers

Association's Automobile Finance Conference, the chairman of Ford Motor Credit said, "Leasing will become as big as the auto industry wants it to be." Some analysts predict that it will eventually account for 40 to 50 percent of new-car and -truck sales. That would make over 20,000 auto dealers very happy.

WHY DEALERS LOVE LEASING

Leasing is popular among dealers for several reasons, all of which have to do with profit.

• First, it generates quicker customer returns to the dealership, since the average lease term of two to three years is shorter than the average new car loan of four to five years.

• Leasing also provides them with a predictable supply of relatively low-mileage, one-owner cars—the bread and butter of a profitable used-car operation.

• *Most important, leasing frequently gives them an opportunity to make more profit than they'd earn on a straight sale of the same vehicle.* That's because most consumers don't understand leasing well enough to negotiate the terms effectively. Here are two examples that illustrate the point:

A friend faxed us the figures for his 3-year lease. It was a done deal, but he wanted our opinion anyway. The details, presented in full on the dealer's summary sheet, showed a capitalized cost of $18,457. Terrific, except for one thing: the full sticker price of the car was $18,302. This friend had "negotiated" a lease in which the price he paid for the car was above the manufacturer's suggested retail price! We told him it was OK, that if he was comfortable with the monthly payment, he should relax and enjoy his new car. But what we were thinking was, "If he were *buying* that car, and he paid the sticker price, would he fax a copy of the sticker and ask what we thought of the deal?"

A student at one of our Smart Car Buyer's seminars came up after the class with two contracts in hand—one for a purchase which didn't happen, the other for a lease of the same car. She had first agreed to buy the car for a net price of $9,500, after subtracting the value of her trade-in. When she arrived the next day with a $9,500 cashier's check, she mentioned to the salesman that she was a real estate salesperson who would use the car for business. Learning this, he said, "You shouldn't buy this car, you should lease it.

That way, you'll get more favorable tax treatment." (Why would anyone take tax advice from a car salesman?) She agreed, and quickly signed a five-year lease on the car. The lease contract showed the capitalized cost: $13,500! They had added $4,000 to the price of the car and made it a five-year term to keep the payments down. Is it just a coincidence that *leasing* rhymes with *fleecing*?

Unfortunately, we hear stories like these regularly. Many people are paying the full sticker price or more for leased cars. They don't realize what's been done to them, because they don't understand leasing. They only understand monthly payments, and the monthly payment on the worst lease deal can be a lot friendlier than the monthly payment on the best purchase deal.

As these two instances illustrate, simply disclosing capitalized costs in leasing contracts doesn't protect the uninformed consumer. In both cases, the paperwork clearly spelled out the size of the rip-off by stating the capitalized cost. But those numbers meant nothing to people who didn't know that the capitalized cost was the price they were paying for the car. And the dealers laughed all the way to the bank.

Many car salesmen will say to you, "What do you care what the price of the car is? You're not buying it, you're leasing it." Nice try, guys, but no cigar. The lion's share of every lease payment you make will pay for depreciation, which is the difference between the price you pay for the car and its value at the end of the lease. And whether you pay the full sticker price or $2,000 less, the value at the end will be the same.

We'll give you all the information you need to avoid a leasing rip-off. But the first question to address is whether leasing represents a viable option for you. Let's examine the issues you should consider.

THE PLACE TO LOOK IS IN THE MIRROR

Leasing can make a lot of sense for some people and be a poor choice for others. Start by asking yourself these questions:

- Do you like to trade cars reasonably frequently, at least every three or four years?
- Do you value the image you project by always driving a late-model vehicle?
- Would you like to drive a more expensive car than you can afford to buy?
- Do you drive an average of less than 15,000 miles a year?

- Would you rather take the cash you'd use for a down payment and put it into an investment that appreciates?

- Conversely, are you someone who can afford to make the monthly payments but doesn't have enough cash for a significant down payment?

- Are you more intrigued with the concept of paying only for vehicle usage than with the psychic rewards some people get from vehicle ownership?

- Are you willing to make monthly car payments indefinitely?

- Do you own a business that will be making those payments?

If you answered yes to most of these, you're a candidate for leasing. Leasing is a viable option for people who trade often and drive a moderate number of miles each year, especially if they can write off most of the payments as a business expense.

If you answered no to most of these initial questions, ask yourself a few more:

- Do you hate making car payments?

- Do you look forward to Car Payment Freedom Day, when you've made your last payment and you get the title certificate from the lender?

- Do you buy new cars infrequently, typically keeping them five years or more?

- Are you someone who likes to squeeze the last drop of value from every dollar you spend?

- Is keeping up with the Joneses relatively unimportant to you?

- Are you someone for whom pride of ownership of a car or truck is important?

- Do you drive significantly more than 15,000 miles a year?

- Do you have enough cash to make a down payment of 20 percent or more on the vehicle you want?

If you answered yes to most of these and no to most of the previous group, you're not a good candidate for leasing.

If you're a candidate for leasing, you'll be pleased to know that you can almost always lease a better car than you could buy with the same monthly payment, and do it with little or no down payment. And frequently, automakers' subsidies reduce lease payments further by offering below-market interest rates and inflated residual values which reduce the depreciation you'll pay for.

If you're not a candidate for leasing, you'll take comfort in the flip side of this fact: The average car loses 65 to 70 percent of its value in the first five years. As depressing as that is, it does say that the average car retains 30 to 35 percent of its value after five years . . . which is 30 to 35 percent more value than you'll ever retain if you always lease your cars.

Although monthly lease payments are almost always lower than the monthly payments for a purchase with conventional financing, leasing is always more expensive than buying in the long run because lessees never own their vehicle. The only way to squeeze every drop of value from the money you spend on a car is to drive it until the wheels fall off. If you pay for a car in four years and use it for eight years, you'll be driving relatively cheap transportation during the last half of its life. And you'll spend much less for the use of a car than someone who leases several vehicles sequentially over the same period.

On the downside, you'll pay the psychic cost of driving a somewhat older car than your less frugal neighbors, the Joneses.

If you're considering leasing, pay close attention to this next point.

AUTO LEASE ADS ARE FINE-PRINT HEAVEN

Let the buyer beware; mouse type was invented for car leases. You'll need a magnifying glass to read the ads, and you'd better use one. Here are some actual fine-print examples (the italics are ours):

- "Lease based on total MSRP including destination charge."

- "Optional equipment not included in monthly payment."

- "Mileage charge of $.15 per mile over 15,000 miles/year."

- "Monthly payment based on *10% down payment.*"

- "Customer responsible at signing for first monthly payment, insurance, taxes, title and registration fees, *plus $450 documentation fee.*"

- "Prices may vary based on dealer contribution."

- "$7,079 *dealer/customer* capitalized cost reduction due at lease signing."

- "*$350 disposition fee due at lease end if vehicle is returned.*"

- "Non-refundable prepaid rental reduction of $1,350 (cap reduction) required."

If leases seem more complex than standard auto loans, it's primarily because the language of leasing is so different from that of buying. And both new-car dealers and independent leasing companies can use that extra layer of "boomfog" to take advantage of leasing prospects.

LEASING BASICS, DEMYSTIFIED

If you like the idea of leasing but are put off by the language barrier, relax. Although leasing has more aspects to consider than conventional financing, it is neither mysterious nor hard to understand. A straightforward walk through the basics should convince you that it's a relatively simple concept that gets tangled in its own underwear by the terminology.

The Simple Concept Think of leasing as long-term car rental. When you sign a lease, you agree to make a specific monthly payment for a specific number of months in return for use of the car during that period. In lease language, you are the lessee, and the company that leases you the car is the lessor. The lessor is typically not a dealer, but a separate company that buys the car from a dealer and then leases it to you. This could be one of hundreds of independent leasing companies or an auto manufacturer's captive finance subsidiary, such as GMAC or Toyota Motor Credit Corporation.

What You Pay For The monthly payments you make to the leasing company cover two basic elements:

• First, you're paying them for the estimated depreciation in the vehicle's value over the term of your lease. You're not buying the whole car; you're paying only for the part of its value that you use. That's why the monthly payment will be lower than a standard auto loan payment.

• Second, you're paying them an interest charge. Often called a lease fee or a lease rate, it's the rough equivalent of a bank's interest charges on an auto loan. You're paying interest on the depreciation, which you are financing and paying off over the term of the lease, just as you would pay off the principal of a conventional car loan. You're also paying interest on the balance of the car's value—what it will be worth at the end of the lease term. That's because the leasing company has to pay the dealer for the whole car, not just the depreciation. Otherwise, you couldn't drive it home. In effect, you're borrowing that lease-end value and driving it around for a few years.

In the language of leasing, the amount of depreciation that you pay for is determined by the difference between two components: the capitalized cost and the residual value. Here's the simple equation:

Depreciation = capitalized cost minus residual value

- The capitalized cost is the equivalent of the purchase price paid when you buy a car. It is the price the leasing company pays the dealer for the vehicle. That amount should be the transaction price that you've negotiated. It can also include other miscellaneous start-up charges, title and registration fees and sales taxes (depending on your state), if you choose to finance them by folding them into the lease and paying for them monthly instead of up front.

- The residual value is an estimate of the car's value at the end of the lease period, frequently stated as a percentage of the vehicle's original sticker price (MSRP). That percentage typically is established by the leasing company, the financing entity that will own the vehicle, and it is not negotiable.

If you think about this for more than five seconds, you'll recognize that the higher the capitalized cost and the lower the residual value, the more depreciation you'll pay for and the higher your payments will be. And, of course, vice versa.

The lease rate or lease fee is the interest rate the leasing company charges you to finance the lease. It is also not negotiable, and it's typically stated as a "money factor," a decimal number used to calculate the interest part of the monthly lease payment. (To convert a money factor to an approximate interest rate, multiply by 24. For example, a money factor of .003125 times 24 = .075, or 7.5%. We'll discuss this in more detail later in the chapter.) The higher the lease rate, the higher the payment. And, of course, vice versa.

Keep It Closed   Most leases are closed-end agreements, which is the only kind you should consider. At the end of the lease term, you return the car and walk away with no additional obligation. The residual value of the vehicle is predetermined; if the car is worth less, that's the lessor's problem, not yours, as long as you've taken reasonably good care of it.

Keep It Repaired   Because the residual value estimate assumes you'll return the car in good shape, you'll pay the cost of fixing anything beyond normal wear and tear. The better leases contain guidelines for acceptable damage, but the definitions can be fuzzy. To be safe, assume that "unacceptable damage" means anything you'd repair or replace if you owned the vehicle. (A dented fender. A broken antenna. An automatic window that won't go down.)

Down Payments   One of the selling points of a lease is that you don't need to come up with a down payment. With many leases, you'll get the keys in exchange for a check covering the first month's payment, the first year's title and registration fees, sales taxes depending on your state, a lease initiation fee and a refundable security deposit equal to about one monthly payment.

But there are lots of exceptions, especially in the most attractive leases. You'll note that the ads for many of those low-payment lease deals have fine print that says something like: "Estimated monthly payment is based on Suggested Retail Price, with a non-refundable prepaid 10 percent capital cost reduction"—otherwise known as *a down payment.* This "cap reduction" pays part of the depreciation charge in advance. Even when no cap reduction is required, some folks might decide to make one to reduce their monthly payments, perhaps by using the proceeds from selling or trading in their old car.

Advance Payment Leases   Some leases offer the option of a single large payment up front that covers all costs for the term of the lease, with no monthly payments thereafter. In effect, that avoids the interest charge for depreciation and prepays the interest on the residual value. These leases tend to be for luxury cars, probably since only luxury-car buyers can write a check that large.

The Purchase Option   You'll have the option to purchase the vehicle for its residual value at the end of the lease term. Going in, you want the highest possible residual value. The higher the residual, the lower the depreciation and the lower your monthly payment. (As we'll discuss shortly, the automakers often subsidize leases by using incentive dollars to establish artificially high residuals.) Even if you plan to buy the car at the end of the lease, you still want the highest residual value. If the buyout price is above the street value of the car, you're not going to pay it ... and neither is anyone else. If you want the car, you'll make them an aggressively low offer, as you would for any used car. Remember, everything is negotiable in this business, and frequently they'll take less if the set price is out of line with reality.

Always check a leased car's street value before you turn it in. Occasionally a vehicle can be worth substantially *more* than its residual value at lease-end. If it is, you may want to buy it and resell it yourself for a quick profit. Note, however, that your state may allow only a brief time period before requiring that you pay the sales tax on the purchase. That means you'll want to have the next buyer lined up before you buy the car.

Excess Mileage Charges   The lease contract will specify a mileage allowance and a penalty for exceeding it. Typical terms: 12,000 or 15,000 miles a year over the term of the lease, and a penalty of 10¢ to 15¢ per excess mile. If you know you'll exceed the limits, some lessors will sell you extra miles at the beginning of the term for a somewhat lower rate, and you'll pay for them with a somewhat higher monthly payment. (But you won't get your money back if you don't use those extra miles.)

Since the terms of most leases are negotiable, you may get the lessor to waive the mileage restriction, reduce the penalty charge or increase the yearly mileage allowance. This is generally not easy to accomplish, but it's worth trying.

There's a happy flip side to this issue. If you drive only 5,000 to 10,000 miles a year, you may quality for a low-mileage discount from some leasing companies, since your car will have a higher value at the end of the lease.

The Lease Term   Most automakers are pushing short-term leases of two or three years, so that you'll be back soon for another new car. What's the best lease term for most people? One that's no longer than the length of the original bumper-to-bumper factory warranty, so you'll never have to face a big repair bill. If you opt for a longer term to lower the monthly payments, you should consider purchasing the manufacturer's extended warranty policy to avoid that risk. (See Chapter 18.) We'd self-insure for a lease term that's only one year longer than the initial warranty, but purchase the extended warranty for anything beyond that.

Early Termination   *Don't sign a lease for a term that's longer than you're sure you'll keep the car.* Every lease has an early termination clause, and it's a painful end to consider. You'll usually have to make all of the remaining payments. (No leasing company will let itself get stuck with a year-old car from a three-year lease contract. The big depreciation hit occurs in that first year, and one year of payments doesn't begin to cover it.) Before you sign any lease agreement, be sure you understand your liabilities in the event of early termination.

Closing the Gap   What happens if your leased car is stolen or totaled in a wreck? All lessors treat a stolen or wrecked car as a form of early termination. Your insurance company pays them the car's market value, but that number can be a lot lower than the amount you still owe on the lease. It's not smart to leave yourself open to this financial risk.

Most auto manufacturers' captive finance companies—such as GMAC, Ford Motor Credit Corporation and Nissan Motors Acceptance Corporation—shield their customers from losses if a leased vehicle is stolen or wrecked, paying any difference between the insurance payoff and the lease balance, and allowing the customer to get a new car. To cover potential losses, they provide their own "gap insurance," either by self-insuring or by paying a modest premium for each vehicle leased (probably under $50 per vehicle). They build this cost into your monthly payment.

Whether you're leasing from one of the captive companies or from an independent leasing outfit, you should ask about *and get* gap insurance. If it's not built into the lease agreement, treat it as a bargaining point and ask them to provide it at no cost. (They may not agree, but it's worth a try.) Gap insurance shouldn't add more than a few dollars to your monthly lease payment. Beware of rip-offs. One large independent leasing company quoted a $100 per month premium on a five-year lease of a luxury car. Clearly, the dealer was an accomplice in this larceny, and the biggest gap there was between the price and the value of that insurance. If anyone tries to pull this on you, walk out and lease somewhere else.

Basic Auto Insurance Costs   You may have to pay more to insure your leased car. Leasing companies tend to require higher limits than many people normally carry. Check this out early and factor it into your cost projection.

Credit Requirements   Most financing companies have higher standards of credit worthiness for leases than for conventional auto loans. If your credit history is spotty, you may not be approved for a lease, or they may require a significant down payment and charge you a higher interest rate.

Sales Taxes   Most states treat leasing like any other purchase and tax the total amount of your payments, including the interest portion. But there are exceptions. Some states make you pay tax on the entire capitalized cost up front, as if you were purchasing the vehicle. (Typically, you may pay it separately or finance it and include it in your monthly payment, amortized over the term of the lease.) If your state has a personal property tax, expect the leasing company to add that in, too. To determine how they tax leasing where you live, call your state's taxing authority or ask your accountant.

These Lemons Don't Make Lemonade   All states have lemon laws, which protect consumers from getting stuck with chronically ill cars. And most of these laws give the lessee (you) the same rights as the lessor.

But why should you have to go through that hassle, when it's the leasing company's lemon? They buy all those cars, so they've got the leverage with dealers and manufacturers. Ask how they'd handle a lemon situation. If you like their answer, get it in writing. If you don't, lease from someone else.

Miscellaneous Fees   The leasing company gets much of its income from fees. The most common one: a *lease initiation fee*, sometimes called a *bank fee*, of $250 to $500. This is typically not negotiable. Then, when you turn in the car, there's often a *disposition fee* of several hundred dollars if you don't exercise your option to purchase the vehicle. This one should be negotiable, all the way to zero. Tell the dealer you won't pay a fee for not buying anything, and that if the leasing company insists, he'd better find another lessor or you'll find another dealer.

FACTORY-SUBSIDIZED LEASES CAN BE VERY ATTRACTIVE

As we noted earlier, people who lease come back for new vehicles more often than people who buy. That's the main reason automakers funnel big incentive money into leases—even those that shun customer rebates and factory-to-dealer cash incentives because they think those things cheapen the perceived value of their brands. Using incentive dollars to reduce monthly lease payments allows them to cut the price under the table, so to speak, without the stigma of open price cutting.

Instead of offering you a $1,000 rebate, or giving dealers a $2,000 cash incentive, the manufacturers take the same sales promotion dollars and shift them over to their captive finance companies. The finance companies use that money in two ways to lower your monthly lease payments. They can raise the residual value to an artificially high level, reducing the depreciation charge. They can also "buy down" the interest rate to a level below the market rate, reducing the finance charge. The net result can be a very attractive deal.

It's not unusual for different vehicles of the same make to have very different residual value percentages and interest rates, depending on how aggressively they're pushing certain models in specific time periods. They usually don't need incentives to sell the most popular products, but when the market is soft you might find special lease deals on almost any vehicle. Manufacturers' different lease incentive programs can come and go like the wind, and tracking them all would be impossible. We know of no reliable source of information on current offerings, but many of them are advertised in newspapers. (*Note:* The factory-subsidized lease deals are not available through independent leasing companies.)

Do You Get the Incentive If You Lease? You might logically ask whether the purchase incentives offered to buyers by automakers are also given to customers who lease. The lessee usually won't qualify for a purchaser rebate because he's not buying the car. But sometimes a manufacturer will state that a rebate applies to either a purchase or a lease. A dealer will usually tell you the truth about that, because the money isn't coming from his wallet.

If it's factory-to-dealer cash, frequently the dealer will get it for a leased car because he'll be selling the car to a financing entity. (Assume that's the case in your negotiations and that the incentive will reduce the transaction price, just as it would if you were buying the vehicle.) If it's a factory-subsidized lease, however, usually there's no incentive for anyone because the manufacturer has used the incentive money to raise the residual value and/or lower the interest rate.

Occasionally, when the lease subsidies are particularly heavy, the dealer may even be required to pay part of the cost. For example, when there's a super-low interest rate, such as 1.9 percent, the manufacturer is selling money at a rate well below the rate it must pay for the same money. In that instance, a dealer may have to contribute several hundred dollars to help defray the extra expense. That's why you'll find some dealers less flexible on transaction prices when super-low rates are in effect.

NEGOTIATING A LEASE WITH CONFIDENCE

Because the key elements of a lease sound like a foreign language to many people, car salesmen can use that language barrier as a smoke screen for some of the most profitable deals in the business. As soon as a prospect mentions leasing, the only thing the salesmen want to talk about is the monthly payment. Often, the first payment they quote is based on the customer paying the full sticker price or more. As we noted earlier, showing the purchase price under the heading of Capitalized Cost may not alert the uninformed. And because the monthly payment on a terrible leasing deal can be a lot lower than one on a good purchase deal, it's relatively easy for consumers to get fleeced if they haven't done their leasing homework.

The Information You Need

The first part of that homework is the language of leasing; the other is the arithmetic. You need to do that arithmetic yourself to be sure they haven't added an extra $30 or $40 a month. Fortunately, it's easy to do if you have the information on these four key elements that determine the size of the payment:

- The length of the term of the lease, typically 3 years or less.

- The capitalized cost, which should be the purchase price you negotiate, plus any additional elements that you agree to include (such as a lease acquisition fee).

- The leasing company's finance charge, expressed as either an interest rate or a money factor. If they give you the interest rate, divide it by 24 (a constant factor unrelated to the length of the lease) to get the money factor. (For example, 7.5%, or .075 ÷ 24 = a money factor of .003125.) If they give you the money factor, multiply it by 24 to get the approximate equivalent of the annual percentage rate (APR) for a loan. (A money factor of .003125 × 24 = .075, or 7.5%.) If the rate is well above the current APR on conventional auto loans at your local bank, you should ask the dealer to shop for a better rate from another leasing company.

- The residual value of the car, or its estimated value at the end of the lease. This will be stated in the lease agreement; it's the price at which you may buy the vehicle at lease-end. It will be shown as a dollar value, but it's figured as a percentage of the gross sticker price (MSRP) before any equipment package discounts. Different vehicles depreciate at different rates, depending on the demand for them as used vehicles. Your monthly lease payment could be lower for a more expensive car that holds its value better than for a less expensive car that depreciates quickly.

The industry's "bible" for residual values is the Automotive Lease Guide's *Residual Percentage Guide.* Published bimonthly, this guide lists each vehicle's estimated wholesale value, as a percentage of the original sticker price, after two, three, four and five years. These estimates assume that you won't buy the car when the lease ends, and that the leasing company will sell it to dealers at an auction. In our experience, the residual values in lease agreements almost always exceed those in this "bible" by anywhere from a few percentage points to 10 or more points, depending on how aggressively manufacturers are subsidizing leases. That means you should view the values in the *Residual Percentage Guide* as low-end, red-flag numbers. If a dealer quotes you numbers that low or lower, you should ask him to shop other leasing companies. To check projected depreciation for the vehicles you're considering, you may purchase the latest issue of the *Residual Percentage Guide* from Chart Software; 800-418-8450. The cost should be about the same as the price of this book.

It's common for different leasing companies to assign different residual values to the same vehicle. When leasing began to grow dramatically, many banks and finance companies lost a lot of money guessing wrong on residual values. As a result, some lessors estimate more conservatively than others. That could cost you money if a dealer sets up your lease with the wrong one.

For example, assume you're considering a three-year lease of a sedan with a sticker price of $22,000. One leasing company estimates a 55 percent residual value of $12,100; another uses 48 percent in its calculation, or $10,560. You will pay that $1,540 difference—an extra $42.78 per month, plus interest.

Tell the salesman that you are aware of these potential differences. You understand that the residual percentage may not be negotiable at any specific leasing company, but you expect him to check several sources to determine which is the most favorable. (As noted earlier, the highest residual often comes from the automaker's captive finance company when incentive money is allocated to the lease deal.)

You have a right to know the residual value number being used. It should be a realistic estimate, not a managed number put there to get more money from you. If it's below the purchase option price listed in your closed-end lease agreement, they're charging you for more depreciation than they project. You should find another leasing deal if they won't change their residual value estimate.

Running the Numbers

Now let's assume you've negotiated a transaction price of $20,000 on a car with a $22,000 sticker price, and that the car's residual value after three years will be $10,000. If you were *buying* it and financing the whole purchase, part of each payment would pay off the $20,000 principal, and the rest would pay interest on the loan. You'd owe $20,000 at the beginning and nothing at the end. On average, over the life of the loan, you'd have an outstanding principal of $10,000—half of the original balance.

When you *lease*, you'll still pay interest on the whole amount because the financing entity (the leasing company) has put up $20,000 to buy the car from the dealer. But unlike a conventional auto loan, the only "principal" you'll pay off is the $10,000 of depreciation—the difference between the capitalized cost of $20,000 (your negotiated price) and the residual value of $10,000. You won't "pay off" that residual value, but you'll pay interest on it because you'll borrow it for the term of the lease.

Now let's do the arithmetic, assuming a 36-month lease with a 7.5 percent interest rate. We'll do it using the constant yield method, which is used by all major leasing companies except Ford Motor Credit.

First, figure the monthly depreciation charge. Divide the $10,000 depreciation by 36 months, and you'll get $277.78.

Next, determine the monthly finance charge. Add the $20,000 capitalized cost to the $10,000 residual value. Multiply that $30,000 by .003125 (the money factor, figured by dividing .075 by 24) to get $93.75. (It appears that we're double-counting the residual value, but we're not. The money factor has a built-in assumption that everything gets paid off, like the principal of a conventional car loan, so it cuts everything in half—assuming that on average, the outstanding "principal" is half of the total. That works for the depreciation, since you will pay it off over the term of the lease. But you won't pay off any of the residual value. So you must double it before you apply the money factor, which will bring it back to its original value.)

Last, add the $277.78 depreciation and the $93.75 interest, for a total monthly lease payment of $371.53. Plus tax.

To calculate the effect of making a down payment or "cap reduction," just reduce the capitalized cost by the amount of the payment and do the arithmetic again.

That's it. Making this relatively simple calculation can be very empowering. With it, you can "solve" for any of the three factors if you know the other two. For example, if you know the residual value and the interest rate but not the capitalized cost, you can try different cap cost assumptions until you find the one that gives you the monthly payment they're quoting. Similarly, you can solve for the interest rate if you know the residual value and the cap cost. Take your calculator with you and run the numbers at the salesman's desk. Chances are, he won't know how to do it. You'll be in control, which is the way it should be.

If there's an exception to every rule, Ford Motor Credit Corporation is the exception on leasing arithmetic. Ford uses an antiquated method to determine lease payments, applying one mysterious money factor to the capitalized cost and another to the residual value. Ford's money factors include a built-in administrative fee which makes the effective APR of the lease 1.5 to

2 percent higher than the "internal" interest rate quoted to you by Ford dealers—a discrepancy that you'll discover when you run the numbers.

There's an alternative method Ford dealers sometimes use to calculate lease payments. They figure the monthly depreciation charge in the standard way, as we have done above. But they perform two nonstandard calculations to figure the finance charge. First, they develop a money factor by dividing Ford's internal interest rate by 12. Then they multiply this money factor by the capitalized cost to get the finance charge. This method also generates a higher effective APR than the constant yield method that is used broadly.

This doesn't necessarily mean that Ford is padding the interest rate. If a dealer quoted Ford's internal rate at 7.5 percent, but the current bank rate on conventional auto loans was 9.0 to 9.5 percent, the company's calculation shenanigans wouldn't really be costing you anything. But if the market rate were also 7.5 percent, you'd draw the opposite conclusion.

About all we can say is that if you want to lease from Ford, that's how Ford calculates lease payments—unless the company switches to the constant yield method, which may happen someday. If that's the bad news, the counterbalancing good news is that Ford pushes leasing very aggressively, frequently with subsidies that could save you lots of money.

Most people will find the simple arithmetic of the constant yield method more than sufficient to help them negotiate a lease effectively. However, if you have computer skills and would like to own software that will perform all the calculations forward and backwards, you should check out the Expert Lease programs published by Chart Software. They enable you to analyze lease terms, perform lease versus buy analysis, compare leases and print payment tables for use during negotiations. One version even contains the Automotive Lease Guide's residual value tables. For current information on specs and prices, call Chart Software at 800-418-8450.

SHOWTIME!

Now it's time to use your leasing knowledge to negotiate the deal. You're going to do it with essentially the same direct, no-baloney approach you'd use to buy the vehicle, outlined in the previous chapter.

First, you'll say that you're going to lease either an Accord or a Camry, you don't really care which, in the next ten days. (Never let them know they've got the only model that makes your heart beat faster.) And you're going to base your decision on price.

Then tell the salesman that you aren't going to talk about monthly payments until you've established the price of the car. And that price will become the capitalized cost of the lease, unless you decide to add other charges to it. Add that you expect them to make a profit, but you're not going to finance their next Hawaiian vacation.

Tell him you've done your homework. You know the dealer invoice price. You know about their holdback. (If there is any, be specific.) You know how sales of that model have been going. (If sales are down, be very specific.) And you've got a good feel for transaction prices among knowledgeable customers. Most important, you know how to do the leasing arithmetic, and you aren't going to sign a lease with any dealership that won't tell you the interest rate or money factor, so that you can run the numbers and arrive at the same monthly payment they're quoting.

Say that if they want to make a fair but modest profit and will deal with you in a straightforward, cards-up way, you're going to be the quickest, easiest lease deal of the month. But you're not going to let them waste your time, and you surely won't waste theirs.

Then make them an offer, using the same basic approach you'd use to buy the car, outlined in the last chapter. Start with the dealer invoice price and add an appropriate number for profit—smaller at first than you're really willing to agree to. Remind them of the specific amount they'll receive in holdback. Then bite your tongue and wait for a response. As we've said before, the person who talks next will lose. If they really want to lease you a car, you should be able to strike a deal with a minimum number of counteroffers. When you reach your target, stand firm.

If they tell you they could sell you the car for that price but can't possibly lease it for the same price, get up and walk out. Many dealers will try to get a higher front-end profit on a leased car because they have fewer opportunities to make back-end profits by selling extended warranties, extra rustproofing and additional accessories, which people are less likely to buy for leased cars. But if they're willing to sell you the car for a certain price, they should be as willing to sell it to the leasing company for the same price. If they're not, tell them you're sure you can find a more cooperative dealership. Just as with a straight purchase, you must be ready to end any lease negotiation abruptly if they're being unreasonable. (Remember Reality 101: You can walk away from any deal, and be absolutely certain there is one just like it, and probably better, around the next corner.)

Once you've settled on price, get the other details of the lease. The lease term, the residual value and the interest rate or money factor, so that you can do your calculation. The lease acquisition fee, if any. The security deposit.

Gap insurance. The early termination penalty. The mileage limitation. Everything you need to know. If the salesman doesn't know the answers, ask to speak to the dealer's F&I (finance and insurance) manager. If they're reticent about sharing all the details, remember that one reason God gave you feet was to walk away from car salesmen. Chances are, they won't let you walk. You're a live sale for them!

Here are a few more suggestions that will help you negotiate the most favorable lease:

RULE 1: AVOID THE DOUBLE WHAMMY; LEASE EARLY IN THE MODEL YEAR

Timing can be as important in leasing as in buying, and the right time to lease is early in each model year. You'll usually get a better lease deal then, for two key reasons:

• First, most auto manufacturers have at least one price increase during the model year. Some have several. If you lease after an increase, you'll have a higher capitalized cost, which will mean a higher monthly payment.

• Second, the later it gets in the model year, the closer you'll come to leasing a car that will be four years old in only 36 months. The numbers go down a little with each bimonthly issue of the Automotive Lease Guide's *Residual Percentage Guide*. Unless the automaker is subsidizing the lease to offset this shrinking value, the leasing company will establish a lower residual value as the model year progresses, which will require a higher monthly payment. This can become a very significant issue if you're considering leasing last year's model after this year's model has arrived. Without big manufacturer subsidies, it will actually cost you more to lease the older model.

So if it's July, August or September, it probably will pay to wait until October, November or December and lease next year's model.

RULE 2: MAKE THEM COMPETE FOR YOUR BUSINESS

How do you get the best lease deal? The same way you get the best purchase deal—by pitting one leasing team against another and discovering which one wants your business the most. To shop smart, you must get specific offers, including all the details, from at least two or three dealers. Assume that all lease deals are negotiable . . . and shoppable.

If you remember only one thing from this book, it should be, *Make them compete for your business.* It always pays to shop around. Even on an appealing factory-subsidized lease, don't assume that the terms in the ad are as rigid as they seem. Contact several dealers for that make and tell them you're going to lease where you get the best deal. Some dealers are always going to be more desperate than others. One might make additional concessions to get your business; maybe he'll lower the purchase price another $500, or waive the mileage limitation, or reduce or eliminate the down payment.

Dealers have a compelling reason to close every lease deal they can: *higher customer retention.* Research shows that about 80 percent of leasing customers return to the same store when they're in the market for their next vehicle. That's more than double the percentage of regular purchasers who return to the same dealerships. This simple fact will give leasing prospects increasing leverage as leasing's share of sales continues to rise.

RULE 3: BEWARE OF THE LOWBALL LEASE OFFER

The lowball opener has found its way to the leasing side of the business. Whenever you see a "no money down, only $179 a month" offer, read the fine print. You may find that it's for a stripped-down model no one would want. The purpose, of course, is to get you into the showroom, where they'll move you to a more profitable model—one with much higher payments.

RULE 4: READ THE FINE PRINT—ALL OF IT—BEFORE YOU SIGN ANYTHING

Signing a lease is like signing a mortgage. You've got to make those payments, or else. Understand exactly what you're signing. If the lessor won't give you a copy to study, there's a reason—one good enough for you to find another, more cooperative lessor.

When you've narrowed your vehicle choices and are almost ready to start negotiating, consider ordering the specific information you need from Fighting Chance. As you now know, you need the same information to lease intelligently as to buy intelligently, and then some. One feature you'll appreciate: a customer service number you can call to ask us to look up residual values in the latest issue of the Automotive Lease Guide's *Residual Percentage Guide.* See Chapter 24 for details.

22

There is no substitute for hard work.

—Thomas Alva Edison

We won't say Edison was wrong. But, considering all the better mousetraps he invented, surely he knew there was more than one way to catch a mouse.

There Must Be an Easier Way!

The problem with doing something right is that somebody's got to do it. We recognize that many of you are sitting there now feeling that this task will require more time and effort than you can give it, wondering if there aren't easier ways to accomplish the objective. You may even be wishing that someone else could do it for you.

As you might expect, we think you should practice what we preach. We're convinced that you can negotiate the best deal yourself, using the methods outlined in this book.

But yes, there are easier ways to buy new cars and trucks. And we wouldn't be providing a comprehensive service if we didn't mention them. Here are four alternatives to consider:

EASIER WAY #1—CARBARGAINS

If you like the idea of having someone else do the hard part (negotiating for you), there's a special service you should know about. It's called CarBargains, and it's offered by the Center for the Study of Services (CSS), a nonprofit consumer service organization in Washington, DC. (As noted in Chapter 14, CSS publishes *CarDeals*, our source of detailed information on manufacturers' current consumer and dealer incentive programs.)

CarBargains is a systematic process in which CSS gets dealers in your market (including one or two you might request) to bid competitively against each other to sell you the car you want. Here's how it works:

1. You can call CarBargains toll-free at 800-475-7283 and tell them the make, model and style of car or truck you wish to buy. They'll charge your credit card $150 for the service.

2. Within two weeks, they will get at least five dealers in your area—including any specific dealers you request—to bid blind against each other for your business. Each dealer commits to a selling price that's a specific dollar amount above or below the factory invoice price.

The participating dealers know that they're in a competition, and that it will take a low bid to win. They also know that CarBargains has a real customer, since anyone who has paid for this service is almost certain to buy a vehicle very soon from one of them.

The Center for the Study of Services has helped thousands of people save money on new cars and trucks via competitive bidding. As you'd expect, they use their solid base of inside information to remind dealers of current factors that give them room to cut prices. Factory-to-dealer incentive programs, manufacturers' holdback and year-end carryover allowances could all come into play in the bidding, depending on each dealer's specific sales and inventory situation. This is also a house sale for the dealer, with no salesman's commission to pay.

3. When the bids are in, they'll send you a report containing a specific price quote sheet for each dealer, showing exactly how far above or below the invoice cost the dealer has agreed to sell the vehicle. The report also includes the name of the sales manager responsible for this commitment. Each dealer's bid must include all the costs involved, including any advertising association fees, processing fees or other miscellaneous charges. You'll have no last-minute surprises.

Their report will also include a printout showing the dealer invoice price for the base vehicle and for all factory-installed options and equipment packages. You'll be able to add the invoice prices for the vehicle and the options you want, then add (or subtract) the amount of the dealer's agreed markup (or markdown). Thus, you'll know the price you'll pay before you leave home.

4. You'll visit one or more of the dealerships, select the car you want and see the sales manager listed on the quote sheet to purchase the car at the price the dealer has already agreed to. The bidding dealers will honor their commitments; they know they won't get future opportunities to bid if they don't. (*Important note*: The Center for the Study of Services has no ties to specific dealers. The only income they derive from the bidding process comes from the consumers who order the service.)

CSS believes that CarBargains frequently results in "the lowest price a dealer will allow," simply because he perceives their phone call as a one-shot, out-of-the-blue opportunity for an incremental sale that he wouldn't normally get.

This strikes us as an attractive, reasonably priced alternative for people who just can't negotiate for themselves. Indeed, CarBargains may be a worthwhile card for any buyer to play. An attractive bid from a relatively unattractive dealership might improve your bargaining leverage with the dealer down the street.

In the next four Easier Ways, you'll do the negotiating, but you won't have to do it in person.

☎ EASIER WAY #2—THE HOUSE SALE VIA TELEPHONE AUCTION

In this approach, you phone your dealer finalists to get bids. (Think of this as your own version of CarBargains.) Ask to speak to the fleet sales manager, not to a salesman. If they don't have a fleet manager (some stores don't), or if the fleet manager deals only with customers buying more than one vehicle, ask for the sales manager. Be sure to write down his name.

When you speak to him, tell him what car (make, model and style) you're in the market for, and that you're going to buy it from some dealer within the next week. Say that you're calling several dealers' fleet sales managers, just once each, to get bids on the car. You'll buy wherever you get the best price, and you aren't going to share one dealer's bid with another. Tell him you know this will be a house sale, meaning there will be no salesperson's commission involved. If it's true, add that you've never talked to any salesman at his store.

Then tell him you've done your homework, and you've got a good fix on what that car will really cost the dealer. You're aware of the factory invoice cost and holdback, as well as any factory-to-dealer incentive programs in effect. You understand that the decision on sharing the dealer incentive is theirs to make, but you're getting bids from other dealers, and you'd expect that the lowest bidder will be sharing a good portion of it.

Next, tell him that to be able to compare apples to apples you're asking each dealership to bid against the factory invoice price. You want to know how much above or below invoice they will charge for the vehicle you want.

You'll ask him about all the charges on the invoice so that you'll know who's including what. Is the destination charge there? How much is it? A dealer advertising association fee? Dealer preparation charges? Will they show you the actual invoice for the car you buy?

Ask whether there are any other charges you'll have to pay that aren't on the factory invoice, saying you won't buy from a dealer that springs a last-minute surprise. Tell him to exclude any customer rebate from the bid. And ask whether they'll honor their bid if they have to exchange cars with another dealer to get the exact one you want.

In sum, what you want from each dealer is a commitment to a number over or under the invoice price, plus a full disclosure of any other costs they will charge for the car you want. If you don't get straight answers from one dealer, call others.

Frankly, we think there's a lot to be said for dealing over the phone, even if you're not conducting this kind of auction. Many Fighting Chance customers have negotiated great deals with no hassle, just by calling the sales manager and being very direct. They pick a target price of, say, $500 over invoice, offer that as a no-dicker price and say that if he agrees to the deal they'll be down within the hour for the easiest sale of the month. (It helps if you know a dealership has the car you want sitting on its lot.)

There are still some dealers who refuse to give serious bids over the phone because they feel they'd be wasting time with window-shoppers. As you know, they want to get you on their turf, in the showroom, where they think they'll have the advantage. It's true that your physical presence as a knowledgeable, disciplined shopper helps establish you as a more serious, more real prospect. But consumers are finding more time-efficient ways to shop for everything, and dealers who won't do business over the phone are losing sales to those who will. And once you've got all the information you need to negotiate effectively, what could be easier than doing it from your own home or office?

EASIER WAY #3—DOING IT BY FAX

Many smart people are using their fax machines to do most of the work. Here's how they do it:

• First they call several dealerships selling the car they want, ask for the sales manager's name (and the correct spelling) and for the dealership's fax number.

• Then, around the middle of the month, they fax a one-pager to each sales manager, describing the car they want in detail (including the specific equipment desired), telling them that next week or the week after, they will be buying it from a dealer either in this city or in the nearest alternative market, which they name. (It's a great idea to say you travel to a second town or city frequently and you don't care where you buy, whether or not it's true. Car salesmen stretch the truth to take advantage of you, so why not turn the tables?) They add that they're quite flexible on color, but not on price, and the dealer with the best price will get the sale. They say they've done their homework and know the invoice price, the holdback and current factory-to-dealer incentives (if there are any). They also say they have a feel for typical transaction prices among informed shoppers. They close by saying, "Fax me information on what you have ready to sell. If a sale by the end of the month works for you to help make your numbers, let me know and price the car accordingly. My fax number is 987/654-3210."

• When they receive return faxes with potentially attractive opening prices, they fax back a note that says: "Thanks for your follow-up fax. I'll be in town Tuesday to make the purchase, visiting the two dealerships I consider most likely to sell the car at an attractive price. Before I leave home, I'll call you with one question: Do you want to see me *first*, because you believe you'll make the purchase so attractive that I won't want to see another dealer, or do you want to see me *second*, because you'll beat any other deal? My fax number is 987/654-3210." (Incidentally, that is a great question to ask, whether or not you're doing it by fax.)

We can't guarantee it, but if you fax half a dozen sales managers, you should get a few promising responses. Dealers can't afford to ignore live prospects, whether they arrive in person or by fax.

EASIER WAY #4—DOING IT IN CYBERSPACE

The popularization of the personal computer is creating opportunities for growing numbers of people to conduct major commercial transactions without leaving their home or office. Surely during the life span of this book, consumers will be able to shop for and purchase new vehicles through online computer services and on the Internet.

As you ponder that option, remember that no matter what medium you use to negotiate with dealers, the only relevant issue is the price. To know whether it's good or bad before you agree to it, you'll still have to do your homework. And even in cyberspace, you'll have to shop dealers against each other to get the best deal.

EASIER WAY #5—THE HOUSE SALE VIA MAIL AUCTION

In this similar approach, with the U.S. Postal Service replacing the phone company on the initial sales contact. First you call the finalist dealerships and get the name of the fleet sales manager and the store's mailing address. Then you mail each sales manager the same letter, requesting that he bid on the car you want.

Your letter will state what you'd say on the phone in Easier Way #2, except that you don't have to spend time establishing the house sale idea. To enhance your chances of being taken seriously as a well-informed prospect, you'll attach a copy of your worksheet. The letter will contain your name and address, as well as your home and work phone numbers. (They are probably more likely to respond by phone than by mail.)

This approach requires a little more advance planning, especially to enable you to take advantage of favorable timing for a factory-to-dealer incentive promotion.

If you mail six of these letters, you should get a couple of interested responses, but you're likely to get better response to phone or fax approaches because they convey a greater sense of urgency.

EASIER WAY #6—AUTOMOBILE BROKERS AND OTHER MIDDLEMEN

Today consumers have the option of paying other people to do their car shopping for them. There are buying services and auto brokers and buyers' agents who will do the job for you. These people charge you a fee for their service—sometimes (if you can believe it) as little as $50 or $100, sometimes a lot more. They negotiate to get a price that's supposed to be much lower than you could get without their help, since they move a lot of metal for dealers.

As you surely know by now, we are convinced that you can do the job very well by yourself, if you have the right information and use it effectively. If we didn't believe that, this book wouldn't exist.

Whether you do it yourself or hire someone else to do it, there's only one relevant question: How good is the deal? The answer will be based on the total price you pay for the car, including the cost of the helper. We believe in most instances the helper's deal won't be that terrific. The major reason for employing any helper should be simply to avoid doing it yourself. You should decide what that's worth to you, but don't go into it assuming you're going to save a bundle, compared to doing it yourself.

In our view, the most attractive helpers are those who work only for you and are compensated only by you. We'd place the CarBargains service (Easier Way #1) at the top of that list because they charge a relatively low fee and you are their only source of income. There's also a growing number of independent buyers' agents worth considering who work only for you and get paid only by you. Their fees are typically higher than that charged by CarBargains, but at least you know whose side they're on.

Then there is the automobile broker, who may charge you $100 or less for his service. But how cheap is that service, and how much does he really save you? Let's consider the low service fee. How do the numbers work for him? Remember, he's got to communicate with you, negotiate with one or more dealers, and coordinate the paperwork and delivery, which he frequently makes himself. All this for only $100?

Assume he sells a car every working day, about 250 a year, giving him a gross income of $25,000, before phone bills. No way, José! Assume he sells two a day, 500 a year, giving him a $50,000 gross. Maybe, but it still seems very skimpy for the work involved.

You won't be surprised to learn that most brokers have another source of income from the deals they make. Brokers are typically in cahoots with dealers and get a silent, undisclosed commission that is often several times the size of the fee they charge the customer. Of course, all of that money ultimately comes from the customer's pocket. This leaves open the question of how much they really save knowledgeable, disciplined shoppers, who might negotiate equally good or better deals on their own.

As one broker reported in a feature story in *Automotive News*, he "sells" 300 to 500 vehicles in an average year, and makes "anywhere from $70 to $80 to more than $1,000 per transaction, depending on the vehicle *and the deal he can cut with a dealer.*" And while all brokers contacted said they always pass along factory-to-consumer incentives, the factory-to-dealer incentives are a different story. As one put it, "We don't get too involved with the dealer's business, we (just) supply them with the audience."

Let's return to the one relevant question: How good is the deal? Assume the car is a popular mid-priced sedan. If the broker gets a $100 fee from you and another $200 to $300 from the dealer, you're starting off $300 to $400 in the hole. And remember, the dealer still wants to make a profit on the sale— at least as much as he's paying the broker, and probably more. So how good can the broker's deal possibly be—especially considering that Fighting Chance customers routinely report negotiating their own deals on popular mid-priced sedans for just a few hundred dollars over invoice?

When you're dealing with a broker, you may simply be trading one car salesman for another. He may have an alliance with the dealer that increases his compensation as the overall profit increases. Our sources tell us these kickback alliances are common, that many buyers can expect surprises like unwanted add-on options—for example, dealer-applied paint sealant that "lists for $750 but will cost you only $225" (and probably costs the dealer only $50). Whenever a negotiator gets the bulk of his income from the firm he's negotiating with, there's an inherent conflict of interest. The broker tells you he's working on your behalf, but he's much more dependent on his long-term relationship with specific car dealers.

Many car-buying services operate much like brokers. They charge you a modest fee, positioning themselves as consumer champions, but have a "sweetheart network" of dealers who are a major source of their income. Some disclose this, but many don't.

In sum, you must draw your own conclusions about these hired guns. Maybe some of them are terrific and others are not. The proof will always be in the result. If the total transaction cost (including the helper's fee) is within the general target price guidelines in Chapter 20 for cars in good supply, you can feel pretty good about the deal. In most cases, we'd bet that you can negotiate an equally good or better deal yourself, if you're willing to put in the effort.

Even if you're not, we believe that an alternative like CarBargains is likely to save you more money than any broker. Why? Chances are that broker is dealing with only one dealer for each make. (Concentrating his business is the main reason he can get good prices, right?) That means, by definition, there's little or no price competition between dealers for your business. And in the retail auto business it's the competitive aspect that enables a buyer to take advantage of price flexibility, which may change dramatically from dealer to dealer . . . and from week to week.

The same principle applies to those fleet purchase referral services that are offered by all kinds of affinity groups. They all claim they'll set you up with a nearby participating dealer whose fleet manager will give you a terrific price.

The problem: He's typically not competing against any other fleet manager. That dealer paid for the privilege of being on that referral list. He doesn't want to compete with anyone for your purchase, which means that you will usually pay for the privilege of buying from him.

The solution: If you use one of these referral services, you should ask for at least three different dealer referrals within your driving radius. And make sure each fleet manager knows he's in a competition.

If we've said it once . . . : Whether you're negotiating for yourself or having someone else do it for you, the key to getting the best deal will always be having several dealers compete against each other for your business.

The buyer needs a hundred eyes,
the seller not one.
— George Herbert

23

Resisting the Final Temptation

Now comes the fun part: uninhibited emotional involvement without financial risk! Driving that new baby home. . . . Being seen by envious friends and neighbors. . . . Inhaling that new-car smell. . . .

Not so fast! There's one more piece of unfinished business, some work to do now to avoid a potential pile of grief next week: *the inspection. Smart buyers allow at least one extra day at this juncture to ensure that they'll be happy with the car they drive home.*

WHAT YOU DON'T SEE IS WHAT YOU'LL GET

That new car or truck belongs to the dealer until the minute you pay him, sign the delivery receipt and drive the front wheels off the lot. If it's got any problems, they're going to get fixed much quicker while he still owns it, before you've given them the final check. (Once you drive away, they can claim that any defect happened after you took delivery.)

Prepare the salesman in advance: Tell him that when the car is ready, you plan to inspect it carefully, and that you'll expect them to correct any problems before you take final delivery. Tell him to be sure to leave the dealer's tags on the car because you want to test-drive it while they still own it. That message should motivate the dealer to pay even closer attention to his checklist for the car before you get there.

MAKE THIS A DAY GAME . . . ON A NICE DAY

You can't inspect a new vehicle properly in the dark or in the rain. Put the trip off until you can do it in broad daylight on a reasonably nice day. Take a friend or relative to help; four eyes and ears are better than two.

Here are the things your inspection trip should cover:

1. Check the odometer. If it shows more than about 300 miles, they'd better have a good explanation. (Maybe they made an exchange with a dealer 200 miles away. But maybe they're trying to slip you a demonstrator that someone's been driving for a few weeks.)

2. Make sure all the optional equipment you ordered is on the car. Then have the salesman take you through the operation of all the equipment—the air conditioner, cruise control, lights, sliding sunroof, stereo system (the basics only for now), electric windows, washer-wipers, remote side mirrors and remote fuel cap opener . . . everything. Make sure it all works. (Incidentally, this is part of his job.)

3. While you're checking equipment, use your accomplice to help check all the lights—the turn signals, backup lights and brake lights, dome light and other interior lighting, even the glove compartment, trunk and engine light (if there is one). Ask whether the manufacturer has set the interior lights to go on briefly when you leave the car at night and, if so, how long they stay on.

4. Go over the interior fabric areas very carefully. On cloth areas, make sure the fit is perfect everywhere, and there are no stains or tears.

Ditto for the carpets and the headliner (it's that cloth or plastic covering between your head and the roof), which should show no sloppy glue stains.

5. Pay close attention to the exterior finish, both body and chrome. It should be perfect, without scratches or dents. (New-car owners should be allowed to put the first "dings" in their own doors.)

If there are small scratches, they can buff them out reasonably easily. *But if the scratches are long enough and deep enough to require repainting, you should refuse the car, period!* The original factory finish is very difficult for even the best body shop to match, and partial-panel matching is next to impossible. They'd probably end up repainting the whole side or panel to fix a small imperfection, and chances are, you'd be unhappy with the result.

6. Check for previous body damage. It's rare with new cars, but it happens—on test drives or in transporting dealer exchanges. Look for mismatched paint on adjacent body parts or ripples in the surface. (Federal law says the buyer must be given a disclosure statement on previous damage.)

7. Check the fit and finish on all things that open and close—windows, passenger doors, hood, trunk, glove box. And make sure all the tires match.

8. While the hood is up, ask the salesman to show you where all the fluids go and how to use the dipsticks to check the levels. The engine oil. The brake fluid. The automatic transmission fluid. The power steering fluid. The radiator antifreeze, and even the windshield washing solution. If any of these is not at the proper level, either the dealer has done a poor job of prepping the car or there's a leak.

9. Most important, take it for a test drive, ideally while the dealer's tags are still on the car, not with temporary or permanent tags assigned to you. That way it's still under his insurance coverage, and he can't claim you've taken delivery.

Drive the car reasonably aggressively to test it. If it's an automatic transmission, do the gears seem to shift smoothly and at natural progression points? Does the cruise control work?

Accelerate to about 30 mph on a straight, flat, dry road with little or no traffic, and take your hands off the wheel. If the vehicle pulls left or right, it may have alignment problems. Slam on the brakes. Does it stop squarely? And find a road with some bumps to drive over to see if there are any annoying squeaks and rattles.

Carry a pad and make a list. Give it to the dealer to copy (keep the original yourself), and tell him you'll come back after they call to say they've fixed everything. At that time you'll examine it again and, if it's perfect, you'll turn over the final check, sign the delivery receipt and drive it off into the sunset. They won't love you for all this, but you will.

10. One last important detail: **Be sure you've communicated with your insurance agent,** so that you're covered the moment the front wheels hit the street in front of the dealership.

Going to a dealer without the Fighting Chance information is like going to the beach without sunblock. You're gonna get burned.
—Tom Gargiulo, Westport, CT

Tom leased his BMW 5-Series sedan for a capitalized cost just $1,190 over dealer invoice. At the sticker price, the dealer profit would have been $7,000.

Call

1-800-288-1134

We cannot tell a lie; this chapter is a commercial. It's for something you'll need, something that others have rated the best of its kind. At $19.95 (plus handling), it's a fine value. You can order it toll-free anytime. And if you find this book valuable, you'll probably want it.

If you've been paying attention, you know that if you're going to shop smart for that new car or truck, you must arm yourself with current information about the model or models you're considering. That information falls into two different areas:

- First, you need the facts about *all* the elements that affect the dealer's bottom-line cost, so that you can determine whether the deal is a good one or a bad one before you agree to it. Those elements are (a) the dealer invoice cost, (b) the factory holdback and (c) any specific factory-to-dealer cash payments that may be available for selling specific vehicles within a specific time frame. (Of course, you also want to know about any customer rebates, which affect your bottom-line cost.)

- Second, you'll bargain from a position of greater strength if you have a feel for how your vehicle is doing in the marketplace and for actual transaction prices among knowledgeable customers. Are sales up or down so far this year? Does the average dealer sell many of that model each month or just a few? Were the most recently reported inventories high or low? Is there a redesigned version of the vehicle coming next fall? And what prices are informed shoppers negotiating, in relation to the invoice price?

Fighting Chance is a unique consumer information service that provides all of this information in one package. We created this business because we concluded that the traditional sources of information were not providing consumers with the information they needed to fully empower them in their price negotiations with dealers. We know of no other source that has put together a package this complete, priced it as a "best buy" value, and made it so easy to order. (Think of this book as the crossbow you'll use and Fighting Chance as the arrows.)

Fighting Chance has been featured in articles in *Smart Money, Reader's Digest, Road & Track, Good Housekeeping, Business Week*, and *Money* magazine, plus newspapers from coast to coast. When the San Jose *Mercury-News* rated the major national car-buying information services, Fighting Chance was the only one to receive four stars. (The *Consumer Reports* Auto Pricing Service got just two stars.)

The three key elements of the Fighting Chance package are described below.

1. COMPLETE DEALER INVOICE DATA

For each car or truck, you'll get a printout showing all the configurations the manufacturer offers, with both the sticker price (MSRP) and the dealer invoice price. That way, you'll be able to make price/value comparisons between different trim levels. (Remember, a higher trim level often represents a better value because it includes standard equipment in the base price that would be extra-cost items in a lower trim level.)

These printouts show the standard equipment included with each trim level. They also include both retail and dealer invoice pricing for all the available preferred equipment packages and convenience groups, as well as the optional accessories and equipment. (Note, however, that a couple of import manufacturers don't share information on pricing for dealer-installed options or accessories. That means, for example, that if you buy one of their models without air conditioning as standard equipment, neither we nor any other pricing service can tell you the dealer invoice price for the air conditioner. In those cases, we tell you what other automakers charge for air conditioning for comparable models, to give you some frame of reference.)

These reports are compiled and updated regularly by H. M. Gousha, a division of Simon & Schuster that has been the definitive source of this information for auto-financing institutions since the 1950s.

Our $19.95 package price includes dealer invoice price data for one vehicle. Complete invoice price information for additional vehicles on the same order costs $8 each. (There's a $3 handling fee on the total order.)

Bonuses

When you order the Fighting Chance package, you'll frequently get a second printout free: the previous price for that same vehicle.

Virtually all manufacturers increase prices during the model year, often more than once and sometimes as late as June or July. As price increases occur, it is common to find identical vehicles on dealers' lots with different sticker prices, reflecting the different invoice prices that were in effect when they purchased the vehicles.

In that situation, it is to your advantage to know the different dealer invoice prices for each vehicle. That's why, if there has been a model-year price increase within recent months, we'll send you two complete sets of pricing data—the most recent price and the price that immediately preceded it.

Here's another bonus: If you're shopping early in the model year and are trying to decide whether to buy the new model or one of last year's leftovers, at your request we'll include the final dealer invoice price for *last* year's model along with the printout for the new one.

We know of no other new-vehicle pricing service that provides either of these additional price printouts. And they can be powerful bargaining tools.

2. *CARDEALS*—THE AUTHORITATIVE REPORT ON CURRENT INCENTIVE PROGRAMS

The second element in the Fighting Chance information package is the latest issue of *CarDeals*, a report covering the current manufacturers' incentive programs—both the consumer rebate offers and any factory-to-dealer cash incentive programs in effect. This biweekly report is compiled by the Center for the Study of Services, a nonprofit consumer service organization in Washington, D.C.

As you might guess, we subscribe to just about everything that covers the retail automobile market, and this is the most comprehensive report available on incentives, by a country mile. *Automotive News,* the weekly newspaper of the industry, has its own incentives section, but *CarDeals* often has twice as many listings—especially in the area of factory-to-dealer cash. (An abridged version of the *CarDeals* report is shown on pages 180–186 of the Appendix.)

Does *CarDeals* include every single incentive that's out there? We'd estimate that it covers over 95 percent of them, but no one could get them all. The automakers don't put this stuff on bulletin boards for everyone to read. The information comes mainly from personal contacts, and there are probably a few they miss—particularly offers only available in limited geographical areas.

Often dealers don't tell their salesmen the full details of these offers, or they tell them less than the whole truth, because they don't want them to negotiate away the factory-to-dealer cash. (We have pulled out the *CarDeals* report in negotiations and watched salesmen's eyes get as big as silver dollars. They've even asked if they may make a copy.) Since you're the one paying for these incentive programs, you're the one who should benefit from them, and you can't negotiate from strength if you don't know the details.

There's another advantage in having a report covering the current incentive offers for all cars: It can open other attractive options. Reviewing the *CarDeals* report, you might discover there's a significant offer on another vehicle you hadn't considered buying—perhaps even a more expensive model than you thought you could afford.

One caveat: This is a supply-and-demand business, and manufacturers generally don't have to spend incentive dollars to move hot-selling vehicles.

An automaker's retail incentives may *average* $500 to $1,000 per vehicle, but many popular cars seldom get incentive dollars. If *CarDeals* shows no incentives for your vehicle, please don't shoot the messenger; we just report the news, we don't create it. Remember, you're also paying us to tell you what *isn't* there, so that you don't end up wondering if the dealer made another $1,000 or so on your deal.

3. OUR BIG PICTURE ANALYSIS— A POWERFUL NEGOTIATING TOOL

As we noted in Chapter 3, there is real power in knowing how the makes and models you are interested in are doing in the marketplace. That's why each Fighting Chance package includes The Big Picture, our written analysis of the current sales and inventory status for each automaker on your list. Updated monthly, these reports enable you to gauge the relative sales strength of different vehicles and determine which are likely to be more flexible on price. You'll also learn whether the average dealer sells thirty of your model every month or just one or two. We'll tell you if there's a major redo of your vehicle scheduled for the next model year. And if there have been changes in a manufacturer's holdback policy, we include the latest information in these summaries.

Perhaps most important, you'll get the benefit of the actual shopping experiences of other Fighting Chance customers. We get continuous feedback from them on actual transaction prices (in relation to the dealer invoice price), and we include this information in our summaries. Understand that this is anecdotal information, not real research. Those that don't feel they have good "report cards" probably don't send them home to us. Nonetheless, if people in several markets report buying a given car for $300 to $400 over invoice, that's strong evidence that you can negotiate a similar deal where you live. We know of no other new vehicle pricing service that provides this kind of insight.

This current perspective can provide real leverage in the showroom. With Fighting Chance in hand, you'll be able to walk in and say, "I know the dealer invoice price of the car I want, I'm aware of the holdback you'll get, and I know about the customer rebate and/or the factory-to-dealer cash offer. I also know that sales of this car are down 10 percent this year, and the average dealer is selling just three a month. And I have a good feel for realistic transaction prices among knowledgeable customers. I expect you to make a profit—a modest one—plus your holdback. If you want to sell an extra car this month and you'll deal in a very straightforward manner, we can conclude this in 30 minutes. Otherwise, I'll go somewhere else."

The fact that *you* know this information—and 99.9 percent of the other shoppers don't (even the salesman probably doesn't know most of it)—stamps you as a knowledgeable prospect who expects no-nonsense treatment. It also changes the way you feel about what you're doing, bolstering your confidence in your ability to negotiate a good deal. As much as anything else, that feeling is what we're selling.

HERE'S A UNIQUE FEATURE: A CUSTOMER SERVICE NUMBER WITH REAL PEOPLE TO TALK TO

Got a question about how to interpret a pricing printout? Having trouble with the leasing arithmetic? Wondering if what that salesman said about a price increase was true? Then you'll appreciate this: Our package arrives with a customer service phone number where you can talk to a real human being.

If you're negotiating a lease, we'll look up the residual values in the latest issue of the Automotive Lease Guide's *Residual Percentage Guide.* (It'll be a toll call, but you'll save the cost of purchasing the guide.) At your request, we'll take out a calculator and go through the lease payment calculation with you over the phone. Some customers even call months later, not having purchased a car yet, to ask if the price has changed or if there are new incentive programs. Just remember that we're in the Pacific time zone, which may be a few hours behind you. Customers only, please.

HOW DOES FIGHTING CHANCE COMPARE TO THE *CONSUMER REPORTS* AUTO PRICING SERVICE?

When we developed Fighting Chance, our objective was to offer a service that was demonstrably better than the existing alternatives.

The most well known and probably the largest auto pricing service is the one offered by *Consumer Reports.* They charge $12 for a printout for one car and $10 for each additional car on the same order. That sounds reasonable, but they frequently treat each different body style and trim level combination as a separate printout. While their reports show the base price for all available trim levels, they often show the optional equipment packages and groups available for only one of the trim levels. To make an apples-to-apples comparison of all trim levels, you must purchase several reports.

By contrast, our printouts cover all the configurations a manufacturer offers for a given vehicle, making it more efficient for shoppers to compare the relative values.

Many Fighting Chance customers have also reported that we frequently have new pricing data well before *Consumer Reports*. For example, Ford introduced the Windstar in the month of March, and we had Windstar pricing by the end of that month. But a customer who ordered on May 6 told us he'd called *Consumer Reports* first, and they still didn't have it.

Customers who use both services frequently tell us that our information is more complete. As an example, one customer reported that *Consumer Reports* told her there was no incentive on Honda Accords, when the *CarDeals* report showed a $1,000 factory-to-dealer cash offer. *Consumer Reports* also told that same customer that Honda had no holdback, when in fact Honda had instituted holdback 10 months earlier!

Although we believe our service is more timely, more complete and a better value, we have great respect for the other work of *Consumer Reports*. Indeed, the annual April auto issue is probably the best single source of information on vehicle safety, reliability, comfort, convenience and economy.

ARE THOSE LITTLE AUTO PRICING BOOKS HELPFUL?

Yes, they can be. Several publishers, including Edmund's and Pace, do a credible job of compiling new-car pricing data. You'll find their paperbacks in bookstores and on newsstands for about $6 to $7 a copy. The problem with these sources isn't accuracy, it's timeliness. They each publish several editions every model year, starting in the fall. If there hasn't been a recent price increase, they're fine. But all publishers need a significant amount of lead time to make changes. Often increases are announced too late to make one edition, and the next edition may be months away. Also, with the model year starting October 1, many people can't wait for these books to hit the shelves later in the fall; they want the information *now*. That's what they get from Fighting Chance.

HOW DO YOU ORDER?

The Fighting Chance information package is easy to order: Just dial 1-800-288-1134, 24 hours a day, 7 days a week. We fill and mail all orders within two business days.

The price of the complete Fighting Chance information package is $19.95, plus $3 for handling, and it includes dealer invoice pricing for one vehicle. Pricing for additional vehicles is just $8 each if you request them on the same order.

We also offer same-day fax service, weekdays only, for an additional charge of $12. If that sounds high, it's because there's a lot of information. The minimum fax is about 15 pages; depending on the number of vehicles, it can easily be double that. Faxing is not a profit center for us, it's a convenience for you. When a fax exceeds 40 pages, we ask if we can please send it via one of the overnight mail carriers. (Fax orders must be received by 3:00 p.m. Pacific time for same-day service.)

You may charge the purchase to Visa, MasterCard or American Express. If you'd rather mail a check, make it payable to Fighting Chance, 5318 East 2nd Street, No. 242, Long Beach, California 90803. (If you live in California, you must add the sales tax of 8.25 percent.)

HOW DO OUR CUSTOMERS RATE US?

The best source of any company's business is customer referrals, and a very high percentage of Fighting Chance's business comes from old customers telling new customers. To illustrate why, here are excerpts from a tiny sampling of the fan mail we receive every day. (We've used initials instead of entire names to insulate the individuals from nuisance or prank phone calls. For the same reason, we don't sell mailing lists of our customers.)

> "The Fighting Chance service saved me literally thousands of dollars. When I showed the car salesman the dealer invoice printout as well as the magnitude of the factory-to-dealer incentive, the price of my Acura Legend fell by over $2,000!"
>
> D. C., Bridgeport, CT

> "When I first read the testimonials of others who used your service, I was a little skeptical and a little intimidated by the whole thing, especially since this was the first new car lease I've negotiated. I thought if I came even close to those results, I'd be satisfied. Well, I got my Saab 900 for $600 over invoice, and it wasn't hard to do. Your advice helped me every step of the way. Spending just $30 and saving thousands of dollars—now that's an exceptional deal! To say that your service delivered is an understatement."
>
> R. S., Santa Monica, CA

"With Fighting Chance, we were able to strip away the salesman's lies and deceptions to get to an excellent final price for our Jeep Grand Cherokee—$275 over dealer invoice. We're very happy. Keep up the good work."

J. F., Augusta, ME

"With the vehicle-specific information from Fighting Chance, selecting and buying a car this time was quite pleasant and not a hassle. Without this information, I would have paid close to $1,000 more for my Cadillac De Ville."

C. W., Richmond, VA

"My wife and I bought an Isuzu Trooper, and the dealer made a net profit of just $600, including his holdback! The information you provided had an enormous influence on the final price we paid. Most significant, however, was the enjoyment I experienced negotiating for a new automobile. Knowledge *is* power, and you are providing an incredible service."

E. W., Atlanta, GA

"I probably saved at least $1,000 by doing my homework and following your advice. The Price Club 'sweetheart deal' was pretty good—$600 over invoice—but I was able to beat that by $200 with your information."

N. R., Santa Monica, CA

"I bought my Toyota Corolla wagon right at the dealer invoice price. You are providing a terrific service."

L. S., Mechanicsburg, PA

"We negotiated a deal for $300 over invoice on the Caravan we wanted. The salesman told us that mail order information isn't always accurate, but your prices matched his invoice to the penny. Easiest deal I ever negotiated."

D. E., Jensen Beach, FL

"The prospect of buying a new car overwhelmed me, and the Fighting Chance material was a godsend. The information empowered me and transformed the task into a challenging adventure. The result: I bought my new Geo Prizm for just $150 over invoice. Thank you for your major contribution to my achievement."

C. S. W., Wooster, OH

"I bought a new Ford Windstar minivan for just $145.15 over invoice, so my modest investment for your service paid off in a big way. You were the only service with information on the new Windstar. (Consumer Reports still did not as of May 6th, and the vehicle was introduced in March.) I used your information about the upcoming all-new Caravan/Voyager to negotiate this deal; no other service gave me this news. Thank you for the most up-to-date information available."

M. A. S., Walworth, NY

"I got my Lexus LS 400 for $2,000 over invoice. Your advice on how to use the fax machine to buy a car worked like a charm. I faxed to 16 midwest dealers and saved over $10,000."

R. S., Green Bay, WI

"It is a wonderful feeling to buy a new vehicle and drive away knowing you got the best deal possible. I purchased my new red Mustang for $278 above dealer invoice. It was so easy it almost scared me. The information you provide is invaluable."

L. Q., Whitesburg, KY

Education is what you have left over after you have forgotten everything you have learned.
                                    —Anonymous

25

The

Executive

Summary

Our objective is to make this guidebook the most comprehensive and useful information package available to people shopping for new vehicles. While it would be impossible to compress it into a pocket-size checklist, we have tried to highlight below the major points covered, for use as a memory trigger as you go through the shopping and negotiating process.

✓ **For openers, have a current overview of the automobile business.** What's the sales and inventory picture for the vehicles you're shopping? The poorer the sales and the higher the inventories, the better the deal is likely to be. (Chapter 3)

✓ **Adjust your attitude.** Project total emotional detachment around car salesmen. ("A car is a car.") Be ready to walk out if you don't like what's happening. Remember, there's always a deal that's as good or better around the next corner. They need you much more than you need them. (Chapter 4)

✓ **Watch all three ways the car store can make money on you:** (1) the price you pay for the new car, (2) the financing and other back-end add-ons they try to sell, most of which are of little value, and (3) the real price they pay for your trade-in vehicle. (Chapter 5)

✓ **Develop a smart buyer's plan.** Learn what your current car is really worth at wholesale and retail. Decide whether you'll trade it or sell it yourself. Shop for money before you shop for cars. Visit car stores to narrow your choices. Gather information on dealer costs. Understand the overall state of the automobile market, including current consumer and dealer incentive offers. Do some homework to choose your dealer finalists. Make timing work for you. Put all the pieces together to approach car stores with an aggressive offer. Play them off against each other to maximize your leverage. And resolve to let them do the stewing. (Chapter 6)

✓ **If you're going to trade, keep the discussion of the price you pay for the new car separate from the discussion of the price they pay for your current car.** (Chapter 7)

✓ **Learn the true wholesale value of your current car before you talk with any car salesman about a trade-in.** (Chapter 8) And sell it yourself if you expect to get top dollar for it. (Chapter 9)

✓ **Deal with the key financing issues before you deal with the dealer.** Shop smart for money, to provide a basis for determining if the dealer's financing proposal is attractive. (Chapter 10)

✓ **Make your tire-kicking and test-driving visits "away games," if you can.** And try to retain two or three equally attractive vehicle alternatives, perhaps by exploring "family relations." (Chapter 11)

✓ **Learn everything you can about what those vehicles really cost the dealer.** Bone up on dealer invoice prices, factory-to-dealer incentives, dealer holdback and year-end carryover allowances. Make a worksheet showing all the elements. (Chapters 14 and 15)

✔ **Make timing work for you.** Try to buy at the end of a dealer incentive program. And in general, gather data early in the month, but negotiate price at the end of the month. (Chapter 15)

✔ **Be prepared for the unexpected, both the games salesmen play** (Chapter 16) **and the high-profit options they'll try to sell as add-ons** (Chapter 17). And determine beforehand if you're a candidate for an extended warranty contract. (Chapter 18)

✔ **Pick your dealer finalists based primarily on service considerations and geography, not price.** Research this issue by talking to service managers, not car salesmen. (Chapter 19)

✔ **Approach the negotiating sessions in a disciplined, confident manner, using your now considerable knowledge base as a lever to keep control of the discussion.** Set a target price based on the guidelines in Chapter 20, but start lower. You don't know where the bone is until you hit it. Be very direct, letting them know what you know and what you expect from them. If they seem unreasonable, show them your heels. There are plenty of other dealers. (Chapters 20, 14 and 15)

✔ **Aim to get all of any dealer cash incentive and all of any year-end carryover allowance.** (Of course, you'll get all of any direct customer incentives, such as factory rebates.) To strengthen your leverage, remind dealers of holdback profits they'll receive later, if appropriate. (Chapters 20, 14 and 15)

✔ **Above all, don't be too eager to make a quick deal.** Nobody's first offer will be his best. Play two or three dealers off against each other, using the phone for follow-up negotiations with your dealer finalists. The secret to winning: Make it competitive every step of the way. (Chapter 20)

✔ **If you're considering leasing, ask yourself the right questions to determine whether it makes sense for you, learn the language, follow the rules in Chapter 21, and read the fine print before you sign anything.**

✔ **If this all seems like more than you can handle, check Chapter 22 for easier ways, particularly the CarBargains option.**

✔ **Be sure to give that car or truck an inspection that would make a marine colonel proud before you give the salesman the final check and sign the delivery receipt.** (Chapter 23)

✔ **Prepare yourself to bargain effectively for the vehicle you want by having (a) a current overview of its sales performance in** the marketplace, (b) up-to-date dealer invoice pricing for the vehicle, including the previous price if there has been an increase, and (c) a list of current incentive activity, including factory-to-dealer cash incentives. You may obtain this information directly from us by calling Fighting Chance at 1-800-288-1134, or you may obtain it elsewhere. But be sure to have it. (See ordering details in Chapter 24.)

Appendix

AUTO MANUFACTURERS' PHONE NUMBERS

If you can't get all your important questions answered by people at a dealership, try calling the manufacturer. Here's a list of their phone numbers. The 800 numbers are typically for customer assistance and information, including direction to your nearest dealer, but you may not get someone who can answer all your questions. If you don't, call the other number, which is for corporate headquarters. Identify yourself as a consumer who is considering the purchase of one of their vehicles and say you have a question the dealer can't answer. The automakers have become much more consumer oriented, and the operators should be able to find someone who can help you. If they can't, perhaps you should consider buying from another company. (*Note*: A few companies don't have 800 numbers, and a couple have only 800 numbers for consumer information calls.)

Acura Division
American Honda Motor Company,
   Inc.
Torrance, California
(310) 783-2000
(800) 382-2238

Audi of America, Inc.
Auburn Hills, Michigan
(810) 340-5000
(800) 822-2834

BMW of North America, Inc.
Woodcliff Lake, New Jersey
(201) 307-4000
(800) 831-1117

Buick Motor Division
General Motors
Flint, Michigan
(800) 521-7300

Cadillac Motor Car Division
General Motors
Warren, Michigan
(800) 458-8006

Chevrolet Motor Division (incl.
   Geo)
General Motors
Warren, Michigan
(810) 492-8841
(800) 222-1020

Chrysler Corporation
(Chrysler, Dodge, Eagle, Jeep,
   Plymouth)
Highland Park, Michigan
(313) 956-5741
(800) 992-1997

Ferrari North America, Inc.
Englewood Cliffs, New Jersey
(201) 816-2600

Ford Division
Ford Motor Company
Detroit, Michigan
(313) 446-4450
(800) 392-3673

GMC Truck Division
General Motors
Pontiac, Michigan
(810) 456-5000
(800) 462-8782

Honda Division
American Honda Motor Company,
Inc.
Torrance, California
(310) 783-2000

Hyundai Motor America
Fountain Valley, California
(714) 965-3508
(800) 633-5151

Infiniti Division
Nissan Motor Corporation in
U.S.A.
Carson, California
(310) 532-3111
(800) 662-6200

American Isuzu Motors, Inc.
City of Industry, California
(310) 699-0500

Jaguar Cars
Mahwah, New Jersey
(201) 818-8500
(800) 452-4827

Kia Motors America, Inc.
Irvine, California
(714) 470-7000
(800) 225-3193

Land Rover North America, Inc.
Lanham, Maryland
(301) 731-9040

Lexus Division
Toyota Motor Sales U.S.A., Inc.
Torrance, California
(310) 328-2075
(800) 255-3987

Lincoln-Mercury Division
Ford Motor Company
Detroit, Michigan
(313) 446-4450
(800) 392-3673

Lotus Cars U.S.A., Inc.
Lawrenceville, Georgia
(404) 822-4566

Mazda Motor of America, Inc.
Irvine, California
(714) 727-1990
(800) 222-5500

Mercedes-Benz of North America,
Inc.
Montvale, New Jersey
(201) 573-2246
(800) 367-6372

Mitsubishi Motor Sales of
America, Inc.
Cypress, California
(714) 372-6000
(800) 222-0037

Nissan Division
Nissan Motor Corporation in
U.S.A.
Carson, California
(310) 532-3111
(800) 647-7261

Oldsmobile Division
General Motors
Lansing, Michigan
(517) 377-5000
(800) 442-6537

Pontiac Division
General Motors
Pontiac, Michigan
(810) 857-5000
(800) 762-2737

Porsche Cars North America, Inc.
Reno, Nevada
(702) 348-3000

Saab Cars U.S.A., Inc.
Norcross, Georgia
(404) 279-0100
(800) 955-9007

Saturn Corporation
General Motors
Troy, Michigan
(810) 524-5000
(800) 553-6000

Subaru of America, Inc.
Cherry Hill, New Jersey
(609) 488-8500
(800) 782-2783

American Suzuki Motor
  Corporation
Brea, California
(714) 996-7040
(800) 934-0934

Toyota Division
Toyota Motor Sales U.S.A., Inc.
Torrance, California
(310) 328-2075
(800) 331-4331

Volkswagen of America, Inc.
Auburn Hills, Michigan
(810) 340-5000
(800) 822-8987

Volvo Cars of North America, Inc.
Rockleigh, New Jersey
(201) 768-7300
(800) 458-1552

ALL-AMERICAN SPEEDSTER

Factory Code No.	Model/Trim Level	Dealer Invoice	Retail (MSRP)
S88	AAA 4-Door Wagon	$15,700	$18,400
S87	AA 4-Door Wagon	$13,000	$15,200
S86	A 4-Door Wagon	$12,800	$15,000
S85	AAA 4-Door Sedan	$14,300	$16,800
S84	AA 4-Door Sedan	$12,200	$14,300
S83	AA 4-Door Sedan	$11,900	$13,900

STANDARD EQUIPMENT BY TRIM LEVEL

A trim level:

Driver-side airbag
Power front disc brakes/rear drum brakes
Dual power mirrors
Digital clock
3.0-liter V6 EFI engine
Full wheel covers
Fuel cap tether
Lights for ashtray, door courtesy, trunk,
    glove box, under hood, headlight
    switch, cargo area, dome

AM/FM radio w/4 speakers
Split bench seats w/dual recliners;
    65/35 split fold-down rear (wagon)
Power steering
Map pockets
P205/70R14 SBR all-season tires
    (blackwall)
Tinted glass
Cloth upholstery
Luggage rack for wagon

AA trim level (in addition to or in place of A trim level):

Deluxe cloth upholstery
Diagnostic warning lights
Remote release, decklid/liftgate

Paint stripe
Cast aluminum wheels

AAA trim level (in addition to or in place of AA trim level):

Air conditioning
Convenience kit
Illuminated entry system
Reclining front bucket seats w/6-way
    power driver seat & lumbar supports
P205/65R15 SBR blackwall tires

Full console w/armrest & storage
3.8-liter V6 EFI engine
Automatic on/off/delay headlights
Speed-sensitive power steering
Tachometer
Luxury cloth upholstery

PREFERRED EQUIPMENT PACKAGES

Factory Code No.	Model/Trim Level	Dealer Invoice	Retail (MSRP)
444B	AA	$1,500	$1,800

Includes 725 manual air conditioning; 757 rear window defroster; 211 f&r floor mats; 129 power door locks; 888 AM/FM stereo radio w/cassette; 254 cruise control; 343 power windows; 298 power driver seat; 765 P205/65R15 tires. Prices reflect discounts of $600 dealer invoice and $730 suggested retail.

(continued)

ALL-AMERICAN SPEEDSTER (*continued*)

EQUIPMENT & ACCESSORIES

Factory Code No.	Item	Model/ Trim Level	Dealer Invoice	Retail (MSRP)
291	Passenger airbag	All	$400	$500
725	Manual air conditioning	A, AA	$700	$850
735	Automatic air conditioning	AAA	$150	$190
525	Antilock brakes	All	$500	$600
754	Cargo cover	Wagons	$ 60	$ 75
254	Cruise control	All	$190	$225
757	Rear window defroster	All	$140	$170
129	Power door locks	A, AA	$210	$250
222	California emissions	All	$ 75	$110
947	3.8-liter V6 EFI engine	AA, AAA	$470	$560
143	Engine block heater	All	$ 20	$ 30
211	Front & rear floor mats	All	$ 40	$ 50
888	AM/FM stereo+cassette	All	$140	$175
861	High-level audio system	All	$250	$300
	(Includes controls for bass, treble, balance, fade; seek-scan turning; AM stereo; Dolby noise reduction; 80 watts power)			
862	Compact disc player	All	$400	$500
	(Includes cassettes; requires 861 high-level audio system)			
311	Power moonroof	AAA	$700	$800
	(Requires 725 manual air conditioning when 735 automatic air conditioning is not ordered)			
298	6-way power driver seat	AA	$250	$300
299	Dual 6-way power seats	AAA	$250	$300
314	Rear-facing third seat	Wagons	$130	$160
301	Leather bucket seats with	AA	$500	$600
	console	AAA	$400	$500
524	Leather steering wheel	AAA	$ 65	$ 90
	(Requires 254 cruise control)			
343	Power windows	A, AA	$300	$360
106	Rear window washer/wiper	Wagons	$100	$150
	(Requires 757 rear window defroster)			
765	P205/65R15 blackwall tires	AA	$130	$150
608	Conventional spare tire	All	$ 60	$ 75
	(Replaces rear-facing third seat on wagons)			
Destination Charges		All	$500	$500

Note: This chart contains fictitious information about a vehicle and a manufacturer that do not exist. It was created solely as an aid in helping the reader learn to build a new-vehicle worksheet, as illustrated in Chapter 14.

CarDeals

Rebate and Incentive Programs Currently Offered on New Cars and Light Trucks

A Newsletter Published by the Center for the Study of Services/Consumers' CHECKBOOK
733 15th Street, N.W., Suite 820, Washington, DC 20005   (202) 347-7283

This is information on deals currently being offered by car manufacturers. Manufacturers sometimes offer *customer* rebates directly to the consumer. You can get the rebate as a check in the mail or you can have the dealer credit the rebate immediately as a discount to reduce the price of your car. A dealer will tell you if any *customer* rebates are available, so you don't have to worry about missing out on something you are entitled to.

Another type of deal offered by car makers is *factory-to-dealer* cash incentive programs. In these programs, the manufacturer gives the dealer a cash payment for every car the dealer sells. Manufacturers sometimes advertise these factory-to-dealer cash incentive programs, but often the programs are secret.

Dealers don't have to tell you about factory-to-dealer cash incentive programs, and a dealer doesn't have to give you any part of the cash incentive payment it receives for selling you a car. Dealers may use these payments for advertising, employee rewards, extra profit, or in other ways. It's up to you to get the dealer to pass all or part of the cash incentive payment along to you. The information this report gives you about ongoing factory-to-dealer cash incentive programs will enable you to negotiate with the dealer.

Here are some tips on using the *CarDeals* information:

• If you are considering several makes/models of cars that seem roughly comparable in value for the dollar, be sure to check whether one carries a rebate or cash incentive program that will significantly drop its cost. It's not unusual for the maker of one car to offer no rebate or incentive program while the maker of a similar car is offering a rebate worth $1,000 or more. That $1,000 may be just what it takes to make the second type of car the best choice for you.

• If a car you want doesn't currently carry any special deals, consider waiting. New programs start all the time.

• To get all or part of the factory-to-dealer cash incentive money that a dealer will receive for selling you a car, you may have to negotiate.

Let dealers know that you are aware of the money and that you intend to shop several dealers until you find one that gives you some or all of this factory-supplied cash.

• Some factory-to-dealer cash incentive programs give dealers larger payments per car as the dealers sell more cars during the program period. Unless otherwise noted, when you see a range in our listing (say, $400–$800), this means that a dealer gets more cash if it sells more cars. In some programs, all dealers have the same volume targets. In such programs, you can expect large dealerships to get larger cash payments than small dealers, because the large dealers sell more cars. In other programs, larger dealerships have to meet higher-volume targets in order to qualify for cash than small dealers have to meet, so there's no reason for you to expect to get a better deal at a large dealership. In our listing, we tell you the programs where incentive payments are "based on sales targets set for the dealer," rather than targets that are the same for all dealers.

• In programs that give dealers higher incentive payments as the volume of cars sold increases, you might do well to delay your purchase until nearly the end of the program period so that some dealers are likely to be at the highest cash incentive plateau.

• If the car you want is part of an incentive program in which payments go up as sales volume goes up, be sure to shop at several dealerships in hopes of finding one that is at the highest payment level.

• In some programs, a dealer that meets a sales target gets extra cash for all cars sold earlier in a period, before it met the target. Since meeting its target may get the dealer hundreds of dollars for each previously sold car, the dealer might give dramatic discounts as it gets close to its target.

• Although you can get a *customer* rebate in the form of a check from the manufacturer, you may be better off to have the dealer credit the rebate as a discount to reduce the price of your car; in some states, doing so will reduce your sales tax.

• Some manufacturers offer reduced-rate financing plans as an alternative to a customer cash rebate. These plans are noted in our listing. You must decide whether the rebate or the finance plan is better for you. The answer depends on the size of the rebate, the factory-offered plan's annual percentage rate (APR), the APRs available from other lenders, the amount you'll be borrowing, and how long a period you'll be borrowing for. On a 48-month loan, each percentage point you cut your APR is the equivalent of a car price discount of about $18.50 per $1,000 of loan.

To illustrate, assume you could get a $13,000, 48-month loan from a bank at a 12 percent APR, and that the special factory plan's rate is 7.9 percent. The savings from using the factory plan would be estimated as follows:

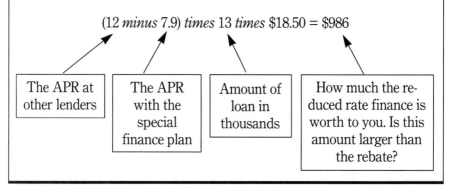

(12 *minus* 7.9) *times* 13 *times* $18.50 = $986

| The APR at other lenders | The APR with the special finance plan | Amount of loan in thousands | How much the reduced rate finance is worth to you. Is this amount larger than the rebate? |

The sample table on the following pages is a shortened version of a CarDeals report. It shows factory-to-customer rebates (followed by a "C") and factory-to-dealer cash incentives (followed by a "D"). The programs run through the date shown in the column marked "End." The CarDeals newsletter typically lists at least twice as many incentive offers. For information on deals on other car types and programs that have ended, or on specific regions, call 202-783-3001.

CarDeals INCENTIVES PROGRAMS

Model	Cash to Customer (C) or Dealer (D) and/or Finance Plan (plans below)	End
SUBCOMPACTS (Current-year models except where noted)		
Ford Escort (last year's model)	$750 (C) or Plan 4 and 5% of list price (D)	9/23
Ford Escort	$400 (C) or Plan 4	9/23
Geo Prizm	$1,500 (C) or Plan 5	9/23
Honda Civic (4-door)	$400 (D)	9/2
Mazda Protegé	$1,400 (C)	9/8
Mercury Tracer	$400-$1,000 (C) (varies by region) or Plan 4	9/23
Nissan Sentra	$1,000 (D)	9/2
Toyota Corolla	$800-$1,000 (D) based on sales targets set for individual dealer	9/2
Toyota Tercel	$200-$400 (D) based on sales targets set for individual dealer	9/2
COMPACT CARS (Current-year models except where noted)		
Acura Integra	$500 (D)	9/2
Buick Skylark	$500-$1,250 (C) or Plan 3 ($500 w/package SA or SB; $750 w/package SC; $1,000 w/package SD or SM; $1,250 w/package SE or SF)	9/23
Chevrolet Cavalier	$750 (C) or Plan 5	9/23
Ford Contour	$500 (C) or Plan 4	9/23
Honda Accord	$500 (D)	9/2
Mazda 626	$1,200 (C)	9/8
Mercury Mystique	$500 (C) or Plan 4	9/23
Mitsubishi Galant	$0-$1,200 (D)	9/30
Pontiac Grand Am	$500 (C) or Plan 1	9/23
Pontiac Sunfire	$0 (C) or ($500 [C] or Plan 1) (varies by region)	9/23
Saab 900	Plan 7 (C)	8/30
Subaru Legacy	$1,000 (D)	11/3
Volkswagen Jetta	$500	9/30
MIDSIZE CARS (Current-year models except where noted)		
Buick Century	$250-$1,000 (C) or Plan 3 ($250 w/package SA or SB; $500 w/package SC; $750 w/package SD or SM; $1,000 w/package SE or SF)	9/23
Buick Regal	$500-$1,250 (C) or Plan 3 ($750 w/package SA or SB; $1,000 w/package SC; $1,250 w/package SD or SM; $1,500 w/package SE or SF)	
Chevrolet Lumina	$1,500 (C) or Plan 5	9/23
Chrysler Concorde	$750 (C) or Plan 2	8/31

(continued)

CarDeals INCENTIVES PROGRAMS (*continued*)

Model	Cash to Customer (C) or Dealer and/or Finance Plan (plans below)	End
MIDSIZE CARS (cont.)		
Dodge Intrepid	$750 (C) or Plan 2	8/31
Ford Taurus (last year's model)	$400–$1,000 (C) (varies by region) or Plan 4 and 5% of list price (D)	9/23
Ford Taurus	$750–$1,000 (C) or Plan 4 plus $0–$180 (D)** based on sales targets set for individual dealer (varies by region)	9/23
Ford Thunderbird (last year's model)	$750 (C) or Plan 4 and 5% of list price (D)	9/23
Ford Thunderbird	$0–$1,500 (C) or Plan 4 (varies by state)	9/23
Hyundai Sonata	$2,000 (C)	10/2
Jaguar XJ-S, XJ6, Sovereign, and Vanden Plas	$3,000–$8,000 (D)	8/15
Lincoln Continental	$2,000 (C)	9/23
Lincoln Mark VIII	$3,000 (C)	9/23
Mercury Cougar (last year's model)	$750 (C) or Plan 4 and 5% of list price (D)	9/23
Mercury Cougar	$0–$1,500 (C) or Plan 4 (varies by state)	9/23
Mercury Sable (last year's model)	$400 (C) or Plan 4 (varies by state)	9/23
Mercury Sable	$750–$1,000 (C) or Plan 4 (varies by state)	9/23
Nissan Maxima	$1,000–$1,500 (D) based on sales targets set for individual dealer	9/2
Oldsmobile Cutlass Ciera	$1,000 (C) or Plan 3	9/23
Oldsmobile Cutlass Supreme	$500–$1,250 (C) (varies by region) or Plan 3	9/23
Pontiac Grand Prix	$500–$750 (C) (varies by region) or Plan 1	9/23
Saab 9000	Plan 7 (C)	8/30
LARGE CARS (Current-year models except where noted)		
Buick LeSabre	$250–$1,000 (C) or Plan 3 ($250 w/package SA or SB; $500 w/package SC; $750 w/package SD or SM; $1,000 w/package SE or SF)	9/23
Buick Park Avenue	$1,000 (C) or Plan 3	9/23
Cadillac De Ville	$1,500 (C)	9/23
Ford Crown Victoria (last year's model)	$1,000 (D) plus 5% of list price (D)	9/23
Ford Crown Victoria	$500 (C) or Plan 4	9/23
Lincoln Town Car	$2,000 (C)	9/23
Mercury Grand Marquis	$500 (C) or Plan 4	9/23
Oldsmobile Eighty-eight	$500–$1,000 (C) (varies by region) or Plan 3	9/23
Pontiac Bonneville	$750 (C) or Plan 1	9/23

(continued)

CarDeals INCENTIVES PROGRAMS (continued)

Model	Cash to Customer (C) or Dealer and/or Finance Plan (plans below)	End
SMALL VANS		
Chevrolet G-Van	$500 (C) or Plan 5	9/23
Chrysler Town & Country	$500 (C) or Plan 2; plus special equipment discounts	8/31
Dodge Caravan	$500 (C) or Plan 2; plus special equipment discounts	8/31
Dodge Ram (wagon, van, conversion)	$1,000 (C) or Plan 2	8/31
Ford Econoline	$1,000 (C) or Plan 4	9/23
GMC Safari	$500 (C) or Plan 1	9/23
Mazda MPV	$1,000 (C)	9/8
Plymouth Voyager	$500 (C) or Plan 2; plus special equipment discounts	8/31
PICKUPS (Current-year models except where noted)		
Chevrolet S-10 Pickup	$750 (C) or Plan 5	9/23
Dodge Dakota	$500 (C) or Plan 2	8/31
Dodge Ram Pickup	$1,500 (C) or Plan 2	8/31
Ford F-Series Pickup (last year's model)	$400 (C) or Plan 4 plus 5% of list price (D)	9/23
Ford F-Series Pickup	$300 (C) or Plan 4 plus $0–$180 (D)** based on sales target set for individual dealer	9/23
Ford Ranger (last year's model)	$400 (C) or Plan 4 and 5% of list price (D)	9/23
Ford Ranger (except Flareside)	$750–$1,000 (C) or Plan 4 (varies by state)	9/23
GMC Sonoma	$750 (C) or Plan 1	9/23
Isuzu Pickup	$800–$1,600 (D)	9/30
Mazda Pickup	$0–$1,400 (C) (varies by region)	9/8
Nissan Pickup	$750 (D) based on sales targets set for individual dealer	9/2
Toyota Tacoma Pickup	$800–$1,200 (D) based on sales targets set for individual dealer	9/2
SPORT/UTILITY VEHICLES (Current-year models except where noted)		
Chevrolet Blazer	$1,000 (C) or Plan 5	9/23
Ford Bronco	$1,000 (C) or Plan 4	9/23
GMC Jimmy '92	$1,000 (C) or Plan 1	9/23
Geo Tracker (2WD models)	$750 (C) or Plan 5	9/23
Geo Tracker (4WD models)	$1,000 (C) or Plan 5	9/23
Isuzu Rodeo (2WD)	$400 (D)	9/30

(continued)

CarDeals INCENTIVES PROGRAMS (continued)

Model	Cash to Customer (C) or Dealer and/or Finance Plan (plans below)	End
SPORT/UTILITY VEHICLES (cont.)		
Isuzu Rodeo (4WD)	$950 (D) or $800–$1,400 (D) (dealer chooses)	9/30
Jeep Cherokee	$500 (C) or Plan 2	8/31
Jeep Wrangler	$500 (C) or Plan 2	8/31
Nissan Pathfinder	$1,000 (D)	9/2
Suzuki Sidekick (2-dr)	$600 (D) or (C)	10/2
Suzuki Sidekick (4-dr)	$300 (D) or (C)	10/2
SPORTY CARS (Current-year models except where noted)		
Chevrolet Camaro	$500 (C) or Plan 5	9/23
Chevrolet Corvette	$1,000 (D)	9/23
Ford Mustang (last year's model)	$750 (C) or Plan 4 and 5% of list price (D)	9/23
Ford Mustang	$500–$1,000 (C) or Plan 4 (varies by state)	9/23
Mazda MX-6	$1,400 (C)	9/8
Mazda RX-7	$2,000 (D)	9/8
Mitsubishi Eclipse	$0–$1,200 (D)	9/30
Nissan 300ZX	$1,000–$2,000 (D) based on sales targets set for individual dealer	9/2
Pontiac Firebird	$750–$1,000 (C) (varies by region) or Plan 1	9/23
Toyota Celica	$600–$800 (D) based on sales targets set for individual dealer	9/2

Finance Plans:

Plan 1 = 6.9% APR up to 48 mos. (3.9% APR up to 48 mos. available on Grand Am and Bonneville—also Sunfire in some states)

Plan 2 = 4.9% APR up to 24 mos., 6.9% up to 36 mos., 7.9% up to 48 mos., 9.9% up to 60 mos. (Minivans: 6.9% APR up to 24 mos., 7.9% APR up to 36 mos., 8.9% up to 48 mos. 9.9% APR up to 60 mos. Lower rates may be available on some models which vary by region)

Plan 3 = 2.9% APR up to 24 mos., 4.9% APR up to 36 mos., 6.9% APR up to 48 mos. (2.9% APR up to 24 mos., 3.9% up to 48 mos. available on Achieva, Cutlass Supreme, Regal, Skylark)

Plan 4 = 7.9% APR up to 48 mos. (Lower rates may be available on some models which vary by region)

Plan 5 = 6.9% APR up to 48 mos. (2.9% up to 48 mos. available on GEO)

Plan 6 = 0.0% APR up to 48 mos. with 40% down payment

Plan 7 = 3.9% APR up to 48 mos. with 25% down payment

Plan 8 = 5.9% APR up to 60 mos. (Lower rates may be available on some models which vary by region)

**If dealer meets targets by end of period gets cash for all cars sold in period.

DOLLAR SAVINGS PER $1,000 OF LOAN AMOUNT

Prevailing
Market Rate
(APR)   Dealer's Factory-Subsidized Interest Rate

2-Year Loan	3%	4%	5%	6%	7%	8%	9%
7%	40.01	30.10	20.13	10.09	—	—	—
8%	49.66	39.85	29.98	20.05	10.05	—	—
9%	59.18	49.47	39.69	29.86	19.97	10.01	—
10%	68.56	58.94	49.27	39.53	29.74	19.89	9.97
11%	77.81	68.29	58.71	49.07	39.38	29.62	19.81
12%	86.93	77.51	68.02	58.48	48.88	39.22	29.50
13%	95.93	86.60	77.20	67.76	58.25	46.68	39.06
14%	104.80	95.56	86.26	76.90	67.49	58.02	48.49
15%	113.55	104.39	95.19	85.92	76.60	67.22	57.79

3-Year Loan	3%	4%	5%	6%	7%	8%	9%
7%	58.16	43.82	29.35	14.74	—	—	—
8%	71.97	57.84	43.57	29.18	14.66	—	—
9%	85.49	71.56	57.51	48.33	29.01	14.57	—
10%	98.74	85.01	71.16	57.19	43.08	28.85	14.49
11%	111.72	98.19	84.54	70.77	56.86	42.83	28.68
12%	124.44	111.11	97.65	84.07	70.37	56.54	42.59
13%	136.90	123.76	110.50	97.11	83.60	69.97	56.22
14%	149.11	136.16	123.08	109.89	96.57	83.13	69.57
15%	161.09	148.31	135.42	122.41	109.28	96.03	82.66

4-Year Loan	3%	4%	5%	6%	7%	8%	9%
7%	75.67	57.09	38.29	19.26	—	—	—
8%	93.34	75.12	56.68	38.01	19.12	—	—
9%	110.54	92.67	74.57	56.26	37.73	18.97	—
10%	127.28	109.75	92.00	74.03	55.84	37.44	18.83
11%	143.59	126.38	108.96	91.33	73.49	55.43	37.16
12%	159.47	142.58	125.49	108.18	90.67	72.94	55.02
13%	174.94	158.36	141.58	124.59	107.40	90.00	72.41
14%	190.00	173.73	157.25	140.57	123.70	106.62	89.34
15%	204.68	188.70	172.52	156.15	139.58	122.81	105.84

(*continued*)

DOLLAR SAVINGS PER $1,000 OF LOAN AMOUNT (*continued*)

Prevailing
Market Rate
(APR)

Dealer's Factory-Subsidized Interest Rate

5-Year Loan	3%	4%	5%	6%	7%	8%	9%
7%	92.55	69.93	46.97	23.65	—	—	—
8%	113.81	91.73	69.30	46.54	23.44	—	—
9%	134.39	112.81	90.91	68.67	46.11	23.22	—
10%	154.30	133.22	111.82	90.09	68.05	45.68	23.00
11%	173.57	152.97	132.05	110.83	89.28	67.43	45.26
12%	192.22	172.08	151.64	130.89	109.84	88.47	66.81
13%	210.27	190.59	170.61	150.32	129.74	108.85	87.67
14%	227.76	208.51	188.97	169.13	149.00	128.58	107.87
15%	244.69	225.87	206.76	187.35	167.66	147.69	127.43

Index

Acura holdback, 80
additional dealer markup (ADM), 84, 95–96
additional dealer profit (ADP), 95–96
additional market value (AMV), 95–96
advertising charge, 122, 125–26
African-American buyers. *See also* minority
    buyers
  price discrimination against, 7
alternatives to negotiating in person
  brokers and other middlemen, 152–54
  CarBargains, 147–48
  by fax, 150–51
  house sale via mail auction, 151
  house sale via telephone auction, 148–50
  on-line computer services and the
    Internet, 151

amortization table, 41–42
annualized percentage rates (APRs), 39, 41
automobile brokers, 152–54
automobile market, 4, 11
Automotive Lease Guide's *Residual*
    Percentage Guide, 52, 139–40, 164
Automotive News, 13, 162
Ayres, Ian, 6–9

bank auto loans. *See* financing
banks, 38
bargaining. *See* negotiating
Big Picture, The, 163
Big Three, basic warranties of, 100
BMW holdback, 79

body damage, 157
brokers, 152–54
Bryan, William, 75
buddy system, 89
bugs in new models, 85
bump-and-grind game, 89–90
buyers. *See also* negotiating; shopping plan;
    shopping without buying; *and other*
    specific topics
  emotional detachment of, 16
  first-time, rebates for, 76
  women, 5–10
buyers' agents, 152
buying services, 152, 153

capitalized cost, 128, 129
  depreciation and, 133
cap reduction, 134, 141
Car and Driver, 55
CarBargains, 147–48, 152
CarDeals, 74–78, 162
  sample, 180–86
carryover allowances, 80, 82–84
  for model-year leftovers of Ford or GM
    vehicles, 116
cash rebates. *See* rebates
Center for the Study of Services (CSS), 74,
    147
certified checks, from prospective individ-
    ual buyers of your car, 35
Chrysler
  carryover allowances, 83
  customer satisfaction and, 108–9
  "family relations" cars, 51
  holdback, 78–79
classified ads for used cars, 32, 33
competitive geography, dealers within, 118
Consumer Bankers Association reports, 39
Consumer Reports Auto Pricing Service,
    159, 164–65
corrosion warranty, 100
cost, dealer. *See* dealer invoice price
credit. *See also* financing (loans)
  lines of, 43
credit life insurance, 44
credit unions, loans from, 40, 43

currently owned car. *See* trade-ins; used
    cars
Customer Satisfaction Index (CSI), 108–11
customer service phone number, Fighting
    Chance, 164
cyberspace, shopping for and purchasing a
    car in, 151

dealer association advertising charge, 122,
    125–26
dealer finance reserve, 38
dealer holdback, 67, 78–80, 97, 115, 121
dealer invoice price (dealer cost), 23, 67, 68,
    121, 122
  in Fighting Chance package, 160–61
  key elements that determine, 66–67
  prices below, 72–73
  target prices in relation to, 114–15
dealer preparation, 95
dealers. *See* new-car dealers; used-car deal-
    ers
demo cars, 116–17
deposit check, salesperson's request for,
    91–92
deposits, from prospective individual buy-
    ers of your car, 35
depreciation, 40
  as hidden cost, 52
  leases and, 129, 131–33, 141
destination charge, 121
detailing your used car, 33
discounts. *See also* incentives; rebates
  for owners of the same make, 76
disposition fee, 137
documents, fee to process, 125
down payment, 22
  deciding on amount of, 39
  in leases, 134

early termination clause in leases, 135
80/20 Rule, 21, 62
emotional detachment, 47, 170
  negotiating and, 16
EPA label, on pickup trucks, 71
European luxury-car dealers, 117

extended warranties, 99–103, 126

fabric areas of car, checking, 156
fabric guard protection spray, 95
Factory Code, 68
factory-ordered cars, 96–98
factory-to-dealer incentives, 72–78, 121
  in *CarDeals*, 162
  factory-ordered cars and, 97
  factory-to-dealer, 23, 67, 72–78
  "prices below dealer invoice" and, 72–73
  timing of purchase and, 82
"family relations" vehicles, 49–51
fax, getting bids by, 150–51
fee to process documents, 125
Fighting Chance information package,
    160–68
  The Big Picture in, 163
  bonuses in package from, 161–62
  CarDeals issue in, 162
  Consumer Reports Auto Pricing Service
    compared to, 164–65
  customer referrals, 166–68
  customer service phone number, 164
  dealer invoice data from, 160–61
  ordering, 165–66
finance and insurance (F&I) managers, 38
finance companies, 38
financing (loans), 22, 37–45, 113, 126, 170
  below-market financing plans, 74–75
  credit life insurance for, 44
  credit union, 40, 43
  dealer's profit for arranging, 38
  "first-time buyer," 39
  home equity, 43
  manufacturer-subsidized, 38–39
  shopping for, 39, 42, 43
  telephone research on, 40–42
  through dealers, 38–39
  20 percent down/four-year rule for, 40, 41
  "upside down," 40
fleet purchase referral services, 154
fleet sales manager, 148–49
Ford
  carryover allowances, 82–83
  "family relations" cars, 51

holdback, 78–79
  incentives for last year's models, 83
Ford Motor Credit Corporation, 38, 44
  calculation of lease payments by, 141–42
  gap insurance, 136
Fortune magazine, 43

game plan. *See* shopping plan
gap insurance, 40, 136
gender discrimination, 5–10
General Accounting Office (GAO), 44
General Motors. *See also* Saturn
  carryover allowances, 82–83
  "family relations" cars, 50
  holdback, 78–79
General Motors Acceptance Corporation
    (GMAC), 38
  gap insurance, 136
Geo "family relations" cars, 51
Gousha, H. M., 70, 161

holdback, 67, 78–80, 97, 115
  when to reveal your knowledge of, 121
home equity loans, 43
Honda, 115–16
  holdback, 80, 165
house sales
  via mail auction, 151
  via telephone auction, 148–50

Iacocca, Lee, 108
imported car dealers, 115–16
incentives
  factory-to-customer, 23, 74–75, 97. *See
    also* rebates
  factory-to-dealer. *See* factory-to-dealer in-
    centives
  for last year's models, 83
  Saturn's policy not to offer, 55
Infiniti holdback, 80
information. *See* knowledge
inspection of a new car, 155–58
insurance, 22, 158
  credit, 44

financing decision and, 39
gap, 40, 136
for leased cars, 136
life and disability, 38
interest charges in leases. *See* lease rate
Internet, shopping for and purchasing a car
    through the, 151
inventory, 13, 14
    estimating how long a car has been in a
      dealer's, 97
invoice price. *See* dealer invoice price
Isuzu holdback, 80

Jaguar holdback, 79
Japanese manufacturers
    basic warranties of, 100
    factory-to-dealer incentives of, 72
    price increases and, 2
J. D. Power and Associates, CSI data pub-
    lished by, 108

keys to your current car held hostage by
    salesperson, 92
knowledge (information). *See also* Fighting
    Chance information package
    homework required to gain, 4
    negotiating and, 3–4
    sales and inventory data, 13

lease initiation fee (bank fee), 137
lease rate (lease fee), 133, 139, 141
leasing (leases), 22, 127–45
    advance payment, 134
    buying and reselling the car, 134–35
    calculating cost of, 140–42
    cap reduction and, 134, 141
    closed-end, 133
    concept of, 132
    credit requirements for, 136
    depreciation and, 129, 131–33, 141
    down payments in, 134
    early termination clause in, 135
    example of negotiating, 142
    examples of bad deals, 128–29
    excess mileage charges and, 135

factory-subsidized, 137–38
fine print in, 131–32
information you need for negotiating,
    139–40
lemon laws and, 137
lowball offers, 145
miscellaneous fees for, 137
negotiating, 138–45
popularity of, among dealers, 128
with purchase option, 134–35
questions to ask yourself about, 129–
    30
reading the small print before signing,
    145
repair costs and, 133–34
sales tax and, 136
shopping for, 144–45
stolen or wrecked cars, 135–36
terms of, 135
timing of, 144
lemon laws, leases and, 137
lessor (leasing company), 132
Lexus holdback, 80
license frame plate with dealer's name, 96
life insurance, credit, 44
lights, inspecting, 156
limited-time offers, 92
lines of credit, 43
loans. *See* financing
logo, car store's, 96
lowball opener game, 90
luxury cars, advance payment leases for,
    134

mail auction, house sale via, 151
maintenance schedule, 52–53
manufacturers. *See also* factory-to-dealer in-
    centives; Japanese manufacturers; *and*
    specific companies
    asking questions from, 53
    phone numbers for, 175–77
    research on women by, 6
    special ordering new cars from, 96–98
Manufacturer's Suggested Retail Price
    (MSRP), 67
market. *See* automobile market

Mazda
   holdback, 80
   Miata, 84
Mercedes-Benz holdback, 80
Mercury incentives for last year's models, 83
Miata, 84
mileage allowance for leased cars, 135
minority buyers
   price discrimination and, 5–7
   stereotypes about, 9
Mitsubishi, 109
   "family relations" cars, 51
   holdback, 80
money factor, 133, 139, 141–42
Money magazine, 43, 44
monthly payments, 22
   automatically deducted, 42
   calculating, 41–42
   for leases, 129–39
   in leases, 22
   not talking to salespeople about, 90
   size of, 39

National Association of Insurance
   Commissioners, 44
National Automobile Dealers Association,
   62
negotiating (bargaining)
   alternatives to. *See* alternatives to negotiating in person
   example of, 118–26
   finalizing the deal, 125–26
   with individual buyers or your used car,
   33–34
   keeping discussion of price, financing,
   and trade-in separate, 113
   leases, 138–45
   psychological aspects of, 15–16
   summary of tips on, 169–72
   unfamiliarity with, 2
   walking out as tactic in, 16, 122
   women and, 9
New Car Cost Guide (Gousha), 70
new-car dealers
   choosing finalists, 104–11
   competition among, 9

within competitive geography, 118
estimating how long a car has been in inventory of, 97–98
number of, for each make, 13
one-price, "no-dicker," 59–64
profit motive of, 9
relatively farther from your home or office, 47
Saturn, 55–58
trades between, 97, 115
new cars. *See also* buyers; negotiating; new-
   car dealers; *and other specific topics*
   bugs in new models, 85
   depreciation of, 40
   new models, 84–85
   price discrimination against women and
   minority buyers of, 6–10
   separating used-car sale from purchase
   of, 26
   in short supply, 117
   special ordering, 96–98
New-Vehicle Worksheet, 68–70
Nissan
   "family relations" cars, 51
   holdback, 79
   Maxima incentive program, 77
Nissan Motors Acceptance Corporation gap
   insurance, 136
nonsmokers, selling your used car to, 32

obnoxious salespersons, 92
odometer, checking the, 156
on-line computer services, shopping for and
   purchasing a car through, 151
opening offer, buyer's, 121, 122
optional equipment and accessories, 93–98
   checking, 156
   listing of, 68
   protection package, 94–95

paint sealant, 95
personal information, salesperson's request
   for, 91, 120
pickup trucks, Monroney label on, 71
Porsche holdback, 80

powertrain warranty, 100, 102
price discrimination, 5–10
prices. *See also* negotiating (bargaining)
   "below dealer invoice," 72–73
   increases in, 1–2, 161
   as negotiable, 2
   "no-dicker," 59–64
   target, 114–17
   value pricing, 63–64
pricing books, 165
   New Car Cost Guide (Gousha), 70
   for used cars, 28, 32
profit
   from leasing, 128
   of "no-dicker" dealers, 60
   from parts and service, 66
   slim-profit deals, 65–66, 113, 114
psychology of negotiating, 15–16

rebates (direct-to-consumer incentives), 74,
   121
   for first-time car buyers or recent college
     graduates, 76
   leases and, 138
   Saturn's policy not to offer, 55
recalls, 85
referral services, 154
release of liability, 35
renting finalist cars, 53
repair costs, leases and, 133–34
repairs, warranty, 105–7
Residual Percentage Guide, Automotive
   Lease Guide's, 52, 139–40, 164
residual value, 139–40
   depreciation and, 133
   purchase option and, 134
Rolls Royce holdback, 79
rust-preventive undercoating, 94–95

Saab, 76
   holdback, 79
sales agreement, reading the, 126
sales events, phony, 87
salespeople, 88–92
   answering questions of, 48–49

buddy system (you and him against
   "them" game), 89
bump-and-grind game, 89–90
deposit check requested by, 91
getting excited about specific cars in the
   presence of, 21
as hostage takers, 91–92
as jugglers, 18–19
keys to your current car held by, 92
knowledgeable buyers and, 3
limited-time offers and, 92
lowball opener game, 90
negotiating with. *See* negotiating
obnoxious, 92
personal information requested by, 91
of same race and gender as buyer, 7, 119
silent treatment from, 89
walking out on, 16, 17
women buyers and, 6
sales receipt, for sales of used cars to individuals, 35
sales reports, 11–12
sales tax, 75–76
   for leased cars, 136
Saturn, 54–58, 118
   bugs in first year of, 85
   competition between dealers eliminated
     by, 55, 118
   resale value of, 56
scratches and dents, 157
selling your used car to individuals, 31–36
service advisors, 53
service departments, 52
   choosing dealer finalists and, 105–11
   CSI scores and, 109
shopping plan, 22–23, 170
   competitive geography and, 118
   creative snooping, 118
   review of, 113
shopping without buying, 46–53
   depreciation and, 52
   "family relations" vehicles and, 49–51
   game plan for, 48
   narrowing your choices, 49
   renting finalist cars and, 53
signing the sales agreement, 126
silent treatment from salespeople, 89

slim-profit deals, 65–66, 113, 114
special ordering new cars, 96–98
special sales events, 87
split-the-difference offer, 123
standard equipment, listing of, 67
sticker. *See* window sticker
sticker shock, 2
Subaru holdback, 79

telephone auction, house sale via, 148–50
test drives
    of car you bought, 157
    of your car, by prospective individual
        buyers, 34–35
timing of leases, 144
timing of purchase, 81–87, 171
    beginning of the model year, 85
    carryover allowances and, 82–84
    end of the model year, 82–84
    factory-to-dealer incentives and, 82, 86
    January and February, 86
    last hour of the last day of December, 86
    last week of the month, 85–86
    new models and, 84–85
    special sales events, 87
    "the middles," 86
Toyota
    dealer association advertising charge, 125
    holdback, 80
trade-ins, 19, 21, 25–26, 113, 170. *See also*
        used cars
    down payment and, 22
    not talking to salespeople about, 91
    at Saturn dealerships, 57
    separating new-car purchase from, 26
trim levels, 68

"upside down" financing, 40
U.S. manufacturers. *See* Big Three
used-car dealers, 25
used cars (currently owned car), 22. *See also*
        trade-ins
    classified ads for, 32, 33
    consumer confidence and demand for, 29
    detailing, 33

keys to, held as hostage by salesperson,
        92
    leased cars as, 128
    negotiating a deal for a new car and,
        126
    pricing books for, 28, 32
    profit of new-car dealers in sales of,
        24–25, 28
    retailed by new-car dealers, 25
    selling to individuals, 31–36
    shopping for offers, 28–30
    telephone research on price of, 32–33
    wholesale value of, 27–30
    wholesaling by new-car dealers, 25

value pricing, 63–64
VIN number (vehicle identification number),
        71
Volkswagen holdback, 79
Volvo holdback, 80

warranties, 52, 99–103
    basic, 100–102
    corrosion, 100
    demos and, 116
    extended, 99–103, 126
    factory-backed, 103
    leasing and, 135
    as negotiable, 103
    powertrain, 100, 102
warranty repairs, 105–7
wholesale value of currently owned car,
        27–30
wholesaling of used cars by new-car deal-
        ers, 25
window sticker (Monroney label), 70–71
    optional equipment and accessories on,
        94–96
    on pickup trucks, 71
women buyers
    bargaining and, 9
    price discrimination and, 5–10
    stereotypes about, 9
    vehicles designed to appeal to, 6
worksheet, 68–70, 119

ABOUT THE AUTHOR

W. James Bragg could name every car on the road when he was three years old, long before he could read. As a teenager his fancy was fueled by a fire-engine red Ford convertible, and he's been an avid student of the automotive world ever since.

Today he is a consumer advocate helping people become more knowledgeable new vehicle shoppers. Much of his counsel is based on the actual shopping experiences reported by the customers of Fighting Chance, the unique information service he founded in 1991. Fighting Chance has been featured in articles in many national magazines (including *Smart Money, Reader's Digest, Road & Track, Money, Business Week,* and *Good Housekeeping*), as well as in newspapers from coast to coast.

A graduate of both Yale and Harvard, he has written on the subject for *Money* magazine and been a periodic commentator on "Marketplace," Public Radio's daily business program.